W9-AQI-155

THE TASTE OF OUR TIME

Collection planned and directed by

ALBERT SKIRA

BIOGRAPHICAL AND CRITICAL STUDY

BY

GEORGES BATAILLE

Translated by Austryn Wainhouse and James Emmons

MANET

SKIRA

Title page:
Le déjeuner à l'atelier (detail), 1868-1869. Neue Staatsgalerie, Munich.

Published by Skira Inc., Publishers, New York, N.Y.
Library of Congress Catalog Card Number: 55-10593.

CHRONOLOGICAL SURVEY

1832 **Birth of Edouard Manet on January 23rd in Paris (at no. 5, Rue des Petits-Augustins, today Rue Bonaparte), son of Auguste Manet, chief of personnel at the Ministry of Justice, and Eugénie Désirée Fournier, daughter of a French diplomat in Sweden and god-daughter of Marshal Bernadotte, later King of Sweden.**

1833 Birth of Eugène Manet, Edouard's brother.

1834 Birth of Edgar Degas.

1839 **Manet a day-boy at the school of Canon Poiloup, in the Vaugirard district of Paris.**

1839 Birth of Paul Cézanne.

1840 Birth of Emile Zola and Claude Monet.

1841 Birth of Berthe Morisot and Auguste Renoir.

1842 **Manet studies at the Collège Rollin, near the Panthéon.**

1842 Birth of Stéphane Mallarmé.

1845 **(or 1846) Acting on the advice of his uncle, Edmond-Edouard Fournier, a connoisseur of art, Manet enrolls in a special course in drawing at the Collège Rollin; here he meets Antonin Proust. His uncle encourages both boys to visit the museums. Manet covers his school notebooks with sketches.**

1847 Thomas Couture scores a great success at the Salon with his "Roman Orgy."

1848 **Completes his studies at the Collège Rollin, having shown, however, little aptitude or taste for learning. His father has his heart set on sending the boy on to Law School, but Manet wants to be an artist. His father will have none of it; heated discussions follow and as an alternative he is allowed to enter the Navy, but fails the entrance examinations of the Naval Training School.**
December 9. Manet goes to sea as an apprentice aboard the transport ship "Le Havre et Guadeloupe."

1848 Birth of Paul Gauguin.

1849 **Manet in Rio de Janeiro.**
July. His final rejection as a candidate for the Naval Training School. His son having returned home with sheaves of drawings in his bags, Manet senior gives in at last and consents to his studying art.

1850 Manet enters Couture's studio in the Rue de Laval (today Rue Victor-Massé), where Antonin Proust joins him. But he soon rebels against Couture's methods. Manet stands out clearly above all the other students.

1851 In December, according to Proust, Manet does a drawing showing the identification of dead bodies at the Montmartre cemetery.

1852 January 29. Birth of Léon-Edouard Leenhoff, son of Suzanne Leenhoff, a young Dutchwoman, born in 1830. Probably Manet was the father of the child. He had met Suzanne Leenhoff in his father's home where she gave piano lessons. Officially Manet was the godfather of the child, who first knew Suzanne as his godmother and later passed as her younger brother.

1853 Birth of Vincent Van Gogh.

1855 At the Louvre Manet copies "The Little Horsemen," a painting then attributed to Velazquez.
At Couture's studio Manet paints a canvas strongly disapproved of by his teacher. His fellow students take Manet's side, congratulate him on the picture and cover his easel with flowers. Couture's retort: "My friend, if you have any pretension to being the head of a school, go set it up elsewhere."

1855 Large-scale exhibition of works by Ingres, Delacroix and Théodore Rousseau at the Paris World's Fair. Courbet exhibits in a pavilion of his own under the banner of Realism.

1856 Probably about Eastertime, Manet leaves Couture's studio. He and Count Albert de Balleroy, also a painter, rent a studio jointly in the Rue Lavoisier. He travels to The Hague, Amsterdam, Dresden, Munich and Vienna, then to Florence, Rome and Venice, haunting the museums.

1856 Duranty launches a review called "Le Réalisme." Courbet paints "Girls on the Banks of the Seine."

1857 Manet meets Fantin-Latour at the Louvre.
In 1857, or thereabouts, Manet and Antonin Proust pay a visit to Delacroix. At the Louvre Manet copies Delacroix's "Dante and Virgil in Hell."

1857 Baudelaire publishes "Les Fleurs du Mal."

1859 Manet's "Absinthe Drinker," painted in 1858, is rejected at the Salon. Delacroix casts the only vote in its favor.

"Boy with Cherries," Manet's first famous picture. It is the portrait of a youngster employed to clean his brushes and scrape his palettes in his studio in the Rue Lavoisier. One of Berthe Morisot's notebooks contains the following entry: " 'Boy with Cherries,' which used to belong to my husband (Eugène Manet). This child, who in despair hanged himself in Edouard's studio, inspired one of Baudelaire's stories."

1860 Troubled by the boy's suicide after he had rebuked him, Manet leaves the Rue Lavoisier studio and takes another in the Rue de la Victoire, only to move on almost at once to the Rue de Douai, where he remains for the next 18 months. He becomes friendly with Baudelaire and paints "Concert at the Tuileries," "Portrait of M. and Mme Auguste Manet," his parents, and "The Spanish Guitar-Player."

1861 "Portrait of M. and Mme Auguste Manet" and "The Spanish Guitar-Player" accepted at the Salon (no Salon having taken place in 1860) and awarded an honorable mention by a very severe jury. In the "Moniteur Universel" Théophile Gautier writes: "Caramba! Here, for once, is a Guitarrero who hasn't come straight out of the Opéra-Comique."

Manet's first meeting with Degas.

"Boy with Cherries" exhibited at the Galerie Martinet, Paris.

1862 Manet moves from the Rue de Douai to 81 Rue Guyot.

In "Le Boulevard," reviewing an exhibition of the Société des Aquafortistes in which Manet showed several plates, Baudelaire wrote about him as follows: "At the forthcoming Salon we shall see several of his pictures, so deeply imbued with a Spanish flavor that one might almost think the genius of Spain had taken refuge in France."

September 25. Death of his father Auguste Manet.

First appearance of Victorine Meurend, later to pose for "Olympia," at the studio in the Rue Guyot.

"Portrait of Baudelaire's Mistress" (Jeanne Duval) and "Le Déjeuner sur l'herbe."

1863 February-March. Exhibition at Martinet's of "The Street Singer," "The Spanish Ballet," "Lola de Valence," "Young Woman in a Spanish Costume," "Concert at the Tuileries"; the latter particularly excites the wrath of the public. March 1. In a letter to Madame Auguste Manet Baudelaire has this to say of her son: "It seems to me difficult indeed not to admire his character quite as much as his talents."

1863 April. Manet sends in to the Salon "Le Déjeuner sur l'herbe," "Mademoiselle V. (Victorine Meurend) in the Costume of an Espada" and "Young Man in the Costume of a Majo"; all are rejected.

May. Opening of the so-called Salon des Refusés, in which these paintings figure. They provoke an unprecedented uproar.

Autumn. "Olympia," for which Victorine Meurend poses.

October 6. Baudelaire writes to Carjat, the photographer: "Manet has just given me the most startling news. He is off tonight for Holland to fetch a wife. There is some excuse for it, however, since it would appear that she is beautiful to look upon, has a heart of gold, and is a very fine musician. So many treasures in a single female—monstrous, isn't it?"

October 28. Marriage of Manet and Suzanne Leenhoff at Zalt Bommel, Holland.

1863 August. Death of Delacroix.

1864 April. Baudelaire leaves for Brussels.

Manet's "Episode of a Bullfight" and "Christ with Angels" unanimously accepted at the Salon. Of the latter Baudelaire writes: "By the way, I understand that it was Christ's right side that was pierced by the spear. In that case you'll have to change the wound before the opening. And take care not to lay yourself open to laughter." But it was too late for any changes. At the same Salon Fantin-Latour exhibited his "Homage to Delacroix," in which both Manet and Baudelaire figure.

June 19. The "Kearsarge," an American man-of-war, attacks and sinks the "Alabama," a Confederate raider, in the waters off Cherbourg. The battle had been expected for several days; the "Alabama" had put in to the neutral port of Cherbourg and was obliged to sail out again after an interval prescribed by international law. Manet probably witnessed the engagement from the French coast.

July. Manet exhibits his painting of "The Kearsarge and the Alabama" in the offices of the publisher Cadart.

1864 Birth of Henri de Toulouse-Lautrec.

1865 Manet's "Olympia" and "Christ insulted by Soldiers" accepted at the Salon. The name of Olympia, probably suggested by the poet and sculptor Zacharie Astruc, is now given the picture for the first time, and against it the full fury of public and critics alike is unleashed immediately.

February. Manet exhibits seven canvases at Martinet's, among them "The Dead Toreador," "Races in the Bois de Boulogne" and "The Kearsarge off Boulogne."

1865 May 11. Baudelaire writes to Manet: "I see I've got to have another word with you about yourself. I've got to make an effort to impress your own value upon you. Confound it, but you expect a lot! It's really fantastic. They laugh at you, do they? Their pleasantries exasperate you... Do you suppose you're the first man to find himself in this situation? Are you a greater genius than Chateaubriand or Wagner? And do you think they weren't laughed at? Well, it didn't kill them. And so as to keep your pride within limits, let me tell you that these two men, each in his own way, are paragons in a period exceedingly rich. As for yourself, you are only the first in the decline of your art. I hope you won't take offense at the rough handling I'm giving you. I'm your friend, you know that. I wanted to get Monsieur Chorner's personal impression. What he had to say of you agrees with what I know to be true: 'He has lapses, shortcomings, he lacks self-assurance, but he has an irresistible charm.' I know all that; I was one of the first to notice it. He added that the picture of the nude, with the colored woman and the cat... is far superior to the religious picture." (Baudelaire probably saw "Olympia" in Manet's studio in 1863 or 1864.)

June. "Olympia" is moved from its original place at the Salon and hung high up on the wall. But a hilarious crowd continues to gather in front of the picture.

August. Manet travels to Spain. At the Prado he sees the Goyas but it is Velazquez he appreciates most. Meets Théodore Duret in Madrid.

October 26. Baudelaire writes to Ancelle: "I've just heard that our excellent friend Edouard Manet has been ill with cholera, but has pulled through all right." On the 28th he writes to Manet: "The first few lines of your letter sent a shiver through me. There aren't ten men in France—surely not even ten—of whom I could say as much."

By now Manet is looked up to as the leader of the non-conformist painters. On Friday evenings in particular Manet and his friends forgather at the Café Guerbois, 19 Avenue de Clichy (today the Brasserie Muller), where two tables are regularly set aside for them: Antonin Proust, Fantin-Latour, Frédéric Bazille, James McNeill Whistler, Nadar the photographer, Zacharie Astruc, Commandant Lejosne (a friend of Baudelaire), Léon Cladel, Edouard Duranty, Armand Silvestre, Renoir (from 1868 on), and occasionally Degas, Monet, Cézanne and Henner.

1865 At the Salon Degas exhibits "The Evils befalling the City of Orléans," a large historical painting.

1866 "The Fifer" and "The Tragedian" being rejected by the Salon jury, Manet shows them at his studio in the Rue Guyot. May 1. Opening of the Salon, while outside a noisy demonstration of rejected painters takes place. Courbet shows his "Forest Covert with Deer" and "Woman with a Parrot," both received enthusiastically by the public.
May 1. Zola writes in "L'Evénement": "Our fathers laughed at Monsieur Courbet, and today we go into ecstasies over him. We laugh at Monsieur Manet; it will be our sons who go into ecstasies over his canvases." After two articles in this vein, his readers protest so violently that Zola is relieved of his duties as art critic for "L'Evénement."

1866 April. Baudelaire is stricken with paralysis.

1867 January 1. In "La Revue du XIXe siècle" Zola publishes a 23-page article on Manet.
A large number of painters have their work rejected at the Salon. Manet submits nothing. Fantin-Latour's "Portrait of Manet" is accepted.
Paris World's Fair. Out of his own pocket Manet spends the equivalent of about 12,000 present-day dollars to put up a wooden pavilion near the Place de l'Alma not far from Courbet's private pavilion. Here he exhibits the following paintings: The Absinthe Drinker, Concert at the Tuileries, The Spanish Guitar-Player, Nymph taken by Surprise, Boy with a Sword, The Street Singer, The Old Musician, Young Man in the Costume of a Majo, Mademoiselle V. in the Costume of an Espada, The Spanish Ballet, Lola de Valence, Young Woman in a Spanish Costume, Le Déjeuner sur l'herbe, Christ with Angels, Olympia, The Kearsarge and the Alabama, The Port of Boulogne, Portrait of Zacharie Astruc, Christ insulted by Soldiers, The Tragedian, Woman with a Parrot, Woman playing the Guitar, The Fifer, Torero saluting.
"Husbands drove their wives to the Pont de l'Alma. Feeling it was too fine an opportunity to pass up, they came to treat themselves and their families to a good laugh. Every 'self-respecting' painter in Paris turned up at the Manet Exhibition. They all went wild with laughter... All the papers without exception followed their lead" (Antonin Proust).
June. Manet paints a "View of the World's Fair from the Trocadéro."

1867 June 19. Maximilian, Emperor of Mexico, condemned to death and executed at Queretaro.

1867 Late June and July. Manet paints the first version of "The Execution of Maximilian" with a view to exhibiting it in his pavilion, but he is forbidden to do so by the authorities.
Summer. Manet stays at Boulogne, then at Trouville.
September 1. Death of Baudelaire. Manet returns to Paris for the funeral, which takes place on the 3rd.

1868 Manet's "Portrait of Zola" and "Woman with a Parrot" (painted in 1866) are accepted at the Salon.
Summer stay at Boulogne: "Le Déjeuner à l'atelier."
Berthe Morisot frequents his studio in the Rue Guyot.

1869 "Le Déjeuner" and "The Balcony" accepted at the Salon.
Eva Gonzalès paints with Manet and poses for him.
Summer. A stay at Boulogne and a trip to London.

1869 Birth of Henri Matisse.

1870 A duel takes place between Manet and Duranty.
At the Salon Fantin-Latour exhibits "A Studio at Batignolles," which shows Manet painting the portrait of Zacharie Astruc while Zola, Renoir, Sisley, Bazille and Monet stand by. Manet exhibits his "Portrait of Mademoiselle E. G." (Eva Gonzalès) and "The Music Lesson" at the Salon.
July 19. Outbreak of the Franco-Prussian War.
September. Manet's family leaves Paris for Oloron-Sainte-Marie in the Pyrenees, while Manet himself receives a commission as a lieutenant. He serves on the General Staff under the painter Meissonier, who is a colonel, and remains in Paris until the surrender of the French armies in January 1871.

1871 The two men having made up their differences, Duranty publishes an article on Manet in "Paris-Journal" in which he praises the painter's work wholeheartedly.
February 12. Manet leaves Paris to join his family at Oloron-Sainte-Marie. On the 21st he goes to Bordeaux where he paints "The Port of Bordeaux." He then visits Arcachon.
May. Manet and his family return to Paris shortly before the end of the Commune.
August. His nerves strained to the breaking-point by the events of the past year, Manet seeks rest and quiet on the Channel coast at Boulogne.
Abandoning the Café Guerbois, Manet and his friends henceforth gather at "La Nouvelle Athènes," a new café on the Place Pigalle in Montmartre.

1871 The picture-dealer Paul Durand-Ruel (who in London during the war had made the acquaintance of Monet and Pissarro and begun buying their pictures) now buys some 30 canvases from Manet, for which he pays over 50,000 francs (over 10 million French francs in present-day money). Manet refuses to include in the deal either "Concert at the Tuileries," "Le Déjeuner sur l'herbe," "Olympia," or "The Execution of Maximilian," for which, as we learn from one of his note-books, he was then asking 6000, 25,000, 20,000 and 25,000 francs respectively.

1871 Birth of Georges Rouault.

1872 At the Salon Manet shows "The Kearsarge and the Alabama," already exhibited twice before and now owned by Durand-Ruel. July. He moves to a new studio at 4 Rue de Saint-Pétersbourg. August. A trip to Holland.

1873 At the Salon Manet shows "Rest" (Berthe Morisot resting on a sofa), painted in 1869 and lent by Durand-Ruel, and "Le bon bock," painted early in the year; the latter is a great success.
July-September. At Berck-sur-mer, where he paints many seascapes, both in oils and watercolor.
About 1873 Manet becomes friendly with Mallarmé.
October 28. Fire ravages the Opera House in the Rue le Peletier, where that same year Manet had made sketches for his "Ball at the Opera." This event leads him to revert to the theme, on which he produces several canvases.

1874 May 14. He submits "Ball at the Opera" and "The Railroad" to the Salon; only the latter is accepted.
In "La Renaissance" Mallarmé publishes an article on Manet.

1874 April 15. Opening of a group exhibition at Nadar's, with works by Cézanne, Degas, Monet, Berthe Morisot, Pissarro, Renoir and Sisley; Manet refuses to take part.
April 25. Reviewing the exhibition in "Le Charivari," Louis Leroy ridicules a canvas by Monet entitled "Impression, Sunrise" and mockingly coins the term "impressionist," which catches on immediately.

1874 Summer. Manet stays at Gennevilliers and Argenteuil on the Seine, where he paints in the impressionist manner and works alongside Monet, producing, among other pictures, "The Monet Family in the Garden."
December 22. Marriage of Berthe Morisot and Eugène Manet.

1874 December 24. A letter from the publisher Poulet-Malassis informs Manet that the engraver Bracquemond has just finished an ex-libris for him: "I don't know whether Bracquemond told you that I originated the design. It wasn't much trouble finding the subject and the motto: it's your bust on a knoll with the words 'Manet et manebit,' a play in Latin on your name, which means 'he remains and will remain.'"

1875 Manet's "Argenteuil" shown at the Salon and warmly praised in articles by Philippe Burty and Camille Pelletan.
June. Publication of Edgar Allen Poe's "The Raven" in a French translation by Mallarmé with woodcuts by Manet.
September. Manet makes a trip to Venice where he paints "The Grand Canal" in the impressionist manner.

1875 Death of Corot.

1876 "The Wash" and "The Artist" being rejected at the Salon, Manet exhibits them together with "Olympia" and other works in his studio in the Rue de Saint-Pétersbourg.
August. A stay at Fécamp on the Normandy coast.
September. "Portrait of Mallarmé."

1876 April. Second Group Exhibition of the Impressionists.

1877 "The Portrait of Faure as Hamlet" accepted but "Nana" rejected at the Salon; the latter is then exhibited in a curio shop on the Boulevard des Capucines.

1877 April. Third Group Exhibition of the Impressionists.
December 30. Death of Courbet.

1878 Manet sends in nothing either to the Salon or the World's Fair exhibition.
June 6. An auction-sale by court order of the belongings of the wealthy collector Hoschedé is a complete fiasco; Manet's "Woman with a Parrot" fetches a mere 700 francs.
July. Manet moves to 77 Rue d'Amsterdam, having been evicted from his studio in the Rue de Saint-Pétersbourg because of the public exhibition he had held there in 1876. Before leaving he paints two canvases showing the Rue Mosnier as seen from his windows.

1879 April. Manet proposes to the authorities of the city of Paris to decorate the Hôtel-de-Ville with a series of decorative compositions entitled "Paris-Halles, Paris-Chemins de fer, Paris-Port, Paris-Souterrain, Paris-Courses et jardins." He receives no reply to his proposal.

1879 Accepted at the Salon are "M. and Mme Jules Guillemet in a Greenhouse," painted in 1878, and "In a Boat," painted in 1874 at the same time as "Argenteuil." Both are praised by Huysmans in an article in "Voltaire."

July 26. "La Revue politique et littéraire" publishes in translation an excerpt from an article by Zola: "Manet seems to have worn himself out with producing too much in too great haste; he is satisfied with the merely approximate; he does not study nature with a true creator's passion." Zola thereupon writes to Manet: "The translation of the passage quoted is inaccurate." The truth is that the translation was as accurate as Zola's criticism was ill-founded.

September-October. Manet follows his first course of treatment at Bellevue. He takes his ailment for rheumatism; what he is really suffering from is locomotor ataxy.

1879 February 11. Death of Daumier.
April-May. Fourth Group Exhibition of the Impressionists; Renoir abstains, successfully showing at the Salon.

1880 April 10. Manet holds a one-man show in the offices of "La Vie Moderne," exhibiting "The Plum," "Monet painting in his Boat" and "Skating," among other works.

Sends in his "Portrait of Antonin Proust" and "Chez le Père Lathuille" to the Salon.

June 19. In "Voltaire" Zola makes amends for the article of the previous year, writing of Manet: "His key position in the transition period through which our French school is now moving will some day be recognized. He will stand out as its most acute, most interesting, most original figure."

July-September. Three months' treatment at Bellevue, where Manet and his family rent a villa. He paints a number of canvases of still lifes and figures in a garden. His letters from Bellevue are decorated with tiny watercolor sketches.

October. His illness has not abated, but he takes up the round of daily life in Paris where he had left it. His wife and mother hold open house on Thursdays and organize small concerts and recitals at which Chabrier, Mallarmé and Clemenceau are frequently to be seen.

Manet does a painting showing the escape of Henri Rochefort from New Caledonia where he had been exiled in 1873 after the Commune. Rochefort had just been pardoned. Manet plans to send this picture in to the 1881 Salon.

1880 April. Fifth Group Exhibition of the Impressionists; Gauguin takes part, Renoir and Monet abstain.

1881 Manet decides to send in no more than a "Portrait of Roche-fort" so as not to rekindle the political scandal touched off by the incident. He also submits a "Portrait of Pertuiset" showing the famous lion-hunter stalking game in a Paris garden with a lion-skin beside him. Many find the picture ridiculous but Manet nevertheless wins a second-class medal for it. This made him "hors concours," which meant that he could henceforth exhibit freely at the Salon whatever the jury thought of his pictures.

Summer. Manet rents a villa at Versailles. He realizes that he is a very sick man, writing to Mallarmé on July 30: "I'm not very pleased with the state of my health since I've come to Versailles." He does two wash-drawings to illustrate Mallarmé's translation of Poe's "Annabel Lee," a few garden scenes and a "Portrait of Henry Bernstein as a Child."

Autumn. Back in Paris he works on "Un bar aux Folies-Bergère."

December 30. Manet finally named "Chevalier de la Légion d'Honneur" thanks to Antonin Proust, now Minister of Arts.

1882 March 24. Election of the jury members of the Salon. In an attempt to blackball them, a list of the 17 painters who had voted the second-class medal to Manet is passed around, but this manœuvre has no influence on the election.

April. Great success of "Un bar aux Folies-Bergère" and "Spring" at the Salon.

Summer at Rueil. Manet has increasing difficulty in walking.

1883 March. Shortly before the 25th, Manet begins his last work, an unfinished pastel portrait of Elisa, Méry Laurent's chamber-maid who had brought him flowers from her mistress.

April 6. Manet is bedridden, having lost the use of his legs. On the 20th he undergoes an amputation of his left leg, but dies on the 30th. He is buried at Passy cemetery on May 3.

1884 January. Posthumous Manet Exhibition at the Ecole des Beaux-Arts. Zola writes the preface to the catalogue. 13,000 visitors between the 5th and the 28th.

1889 At the Paris World's Fair exhibition 15 paintings by Manet, including "Olympia," are the object of general admiration.

1890 "Olympia" is purchased from Manet's widow by public subscription and offered to the state. Refused by the Louvre, it is hung in the Luxembourg Museum. It was transferred to the Louvre in 1907 by Clemenceau, then Prime Minister.

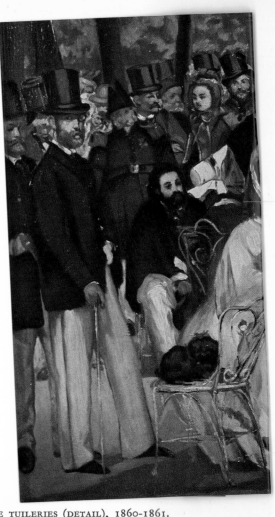

CONCERT AT THE TUILERIES (DETAIL), 1860-1861.
BY COURTESY OF THE TRUSTEES, NATIONAL GALLERY, LONDON.

MANET, GENTLEMAN ARTIST

Manet has a place all his own in the history of art. Not only was he a very great painter, but he cut himself off from the painters who preceded him, opening up the age we live in today, the age we call Modern Times. Completely out of step with his own, he shocked and scandalized his contemporaries, to whom his painting came like a bolt out of the blue. The word "revolution" might describe this irruption and the completely new outlook behind it, were it not for the misleading political implications almost inseparable from such a word.

The difference between Manet and the other artists of his day can be summed up in two points.

First, a Manet canvas, by its very nature, conflicted with everything that a painting was, at the time, commonly expected to be. Duranty, a critic of the period, stated the case as follows: "At any exhibition," he wrote in 1870, "even from many rooms away, there is only one painting that stands out from all the rest: it's a Manet every time. One is apt to laugh, for the effect is queer when a single thing differs from all the others."

The second point to be made is no less arresting. Never prior to Manet had the breach between the taste of the public and changing types of beauty—which art continually renews—been so conclusively final. With Manet began the days of wrath, of those outbursts of scorn and derision with which, ever since, the public has greeted each successive rejuvenation of beauty. Others before him had roused indignation; the relative unity of classical taste had been all but shattered by Romanticism, while Delacroix, Courbet, and even Ingres, for all his classicism, had set the public laughing. But the laughter that lay in wait for *Olympia* was something unprecedented; here was the first masterpiece before which the crowd fairly lost all control of itself.

This state of affairs was doubly paradoxical in view of Manet's mild-mannered, self-effacing character. Yet as early as February 1863, only a few weeks after his thirty-first birthday, with the showing of his *Concert at the Tuileries* at the Galerie Martinet, Manet got his first taste of notoriety; then in May, at the Salon des Refusés, he touched off a scandal that reached its peak in the uproar over *Olympia* at the 1865 Salon and indeed threatened to get out of hand. Degas, only two years his junior, had yet to show anything like the same originality, and at the 1865 Salon exhibited a hopelessly dull, hopelessly conventional historical painting entitled *The Evils befalling the City of Orléans*. The fact remains that there is a richness in Degas' personality that Manet's lacks. A gentleman painter, a man about town, Manet only skimmed the surface of some of the more vital things of life. The portraits and photographs we have of him fail to excite our interest. The things he had to say—as recorded by Antonin Proust and by Baudelaire in *La Corde*—amount to little more than small talk, lit up now and then by a flash of wit or plain common sense.

Manet was much amused at the efforts being made to bring historical figures back to life in painting. "Do you suppose you can paint a man with only his hunting licence to go on?" he said to Proust, adding: "There's only one way of going about it. Take a look and then put down what you see, straightaway. If you've got it, good. If you haven't, start again. All the rest is nonsense." And again in Baudelaire's prose-poem *La Corde* (Manet is not named but there can be no doubt that he is the speaker): "As a painter I am called upon to look hard at the faces that cross my path, and you know the delight we take in this faculty of ours which, in our eyes, makes life more alive and more meaningful than it is for other men."

It is in his friendships—and in his paintings—rather than in his conversation that we detect a yearning for poetry behind this pleasant, easy-going exterior. Manet was a friend, one of the closest friends, first of Baudelaire, then of Mallarmé; with the latter he maintained an almost daily contact which only ended with death. We get some idea of Manet's double nature, shy and passionate, from a letter Baudelaire wrote to Théophile Thoré (June 20, 1864): "Monsieur Manet, generally regarded as either a madman or a crank, is simply a very honest, very straightforward person, doing his utmost to be reasonable, but unfortunately marked by romanticism from birth."

Manet, as I am inclined to think of him, was consumed by a creative fever that literally fed on poetry; that was the inner man, masked by an outward show of urbanity. Though admitting to Zola that he "reveled in society life and took exquisite pleasure in the glitter and fragrance of evening parties," Manet, man of the world and brilliant tattler that he was, felt truly at home, not in magnificent surroundings, but in the cafés, which were then as essential in the life of a Parisian who sought intellectual company as were the races in the life of the "smart set." He sometimes went to the fashionable Café Tortoni, but more often to the Café Guerbois, a less pretentious place where he hobnobbed with writers and artists; there the management set aside a table in the evening for Manet and his friends. He passed for something of a wit and Clemenceau, whose portrait he painted and who himself was noted for his caustic tongue, used to tell how much he enjoyed chatting with Manet—"Such a witty fellow he was!" But in the morning his studio was waiting for him; then began "the fury with which he flung himself at the bare canvas, pell-mell, as if he had never painted before." And in the morning Mallarmé used to drop in and watch the outpouring of this passion for some indefinable thing his feverish hand strove to capture. Afterwards came the relaxation of friendly gatherings in the cafés.

PORTRAIT OF EMILE ZOLA, 1868. (74¾ × 43¼ ˝)
LOUVRE, PARIS.

The sculptor, poet and critic Zacharie Astruc and the novelist Emile Zola loyally defended Manet at the very time, in the mid-sixties, when for public, critics and academicians alike his every work was anathema. The fine, full-syllabled name of "Olympia" comes from a Baudelairian poem by Astruc: *Quand, lasse de rêver, Olympia sommeille...* Braving the storm that broke over Manet's head when that famous picture was exhibited in 1865, Zola imperturbably, prophetically wrote: "Monsieur Manet's place is in the Louvre."

PORTRAIT OF ZACHARIE ASTRUC, 1864. (35 ½ × 45 ½")
KUNSTHALLE, BREMEN.

Manet had nothing very profound to say, nor was there anything very striking about his appearance. Not the man to make a show of the storm that raged within him, he quietly went about his work of preparing the way for a new art.

He was of medium height. "Whether in the country or in town," said Antonin Proust, his boyhood friend, "he invariably wore a coat or a jacket nipped in at the waist, with light-colored trousers and a very tall, wide-brimmed hat." "A beard and thinning blond hair, greying with elegance," said Mallarmé. And Zola: "Keen, intelligent eyes, a restless mouth turning ironic now and again; the whole of his expressive, irregular face has an indefinable finesse and vigor about it."

"He walked with a jaunt," said Proust of young Manet, "to which something loose and easy in his gait gave a particular kind of elegance. However much he overdid it, emphasizing his slouch and affecting the drawling accent of a young Parisian, he never quite managed to be really vulgar... Few men have been more charming then he." Such was Manet till the end of his life.

Here is a thumbnail sketch of him written in 1881, when Manet was nearly fifty and had become a typically Parisian figure: "His head and hat thrown well back, his chin held in the air, looking down more with his nose than with his eyes, whose glassy coolness is kindled by indomitable will-power; a quizzical, skeptical mouth parts in the middle above a blond beard trimmed fanwise. Sporting yellow gloves, a fresh cravat, expensive shoes, light-colored trousers, a flower in his button-hole, so you find him pacing down the Boulevard des Italiens with the brisk step of a man hurrying to a rendez-vous with a pretty woman, or seated on the terrace of the Café Riche or Tortoni's, a fine cigar between his lips and a high-priced drink on the table in front of him."

SELF-PORTRAIT WITH PALETTE, 1879. $(33\frac{1}{2} \times 27\frac{1}{2}")$
JAKOB GOLDSCHMIDT COLLECTION, NEW YORK.

23

He was a man of the world, and made no secret of it. Yet his aplomb concealed a rankling bitterness. Few more charming men than he, yet few have suffered more not simply from their failure to gain recognition, but from being a target of public ridicule. Baudelaire felt moved to take him to task for this. "Confound it!" he exclaimed, "but you expect a lot! It's really fantastic." One of Berthe Morisot's letters describes him as embittered to the very end by the blind incomprehension of the art public.

His outward calm was by no means impassible, since he went so far as to challenge his friend Duranty to a duel. The latter, a well-known novelist and critic, and an advocate of realism in the arts, had published a rather chilly article in *Paris-Journal*. Manet took offense at this, strode up to Duranty's table at the Café Guerbois that very evening and slapped him. "A single engagement took place," the police records report, "and it was of such violence that both swords were badly bent. Monsieur Duranty received a slight wound below his right breast, his opponent's sword having glanced his side." But the two men patched up their quarrel and a few months later Duranty wrote a glowing article on Manet (quoted above in part) which put a fresh seal on their friendship, momentarily troubled by ill-temper.

Behind the façade of well-mannered self-assurance, then, we glimpse a man vulnerable, temperamental, impulsive. But this instability is quite in keeping with the impersonal character of the one venture, the one risk, to which he exposed himself. In fact there is something impersonal and aloof about Manet's entire life. A little superficial perhaps, but driven on by inner forces that gave him no rest, Manet was possessed by a desire for something beyond his reach which he never fully understood and which left him for ever tantalized and unsatisfied, on the brink of nervous exhaustion.

This picture is a landmark in the history of modern art and literature. It is also a memorial, made to last, to the friendship uniting two great minds, a poet's and a painter's. Into the huge space of this small canvas no reverberation of lesser men's frailties could intrude. Here all is the powerful lightness of the soaring spirit, the "swinging crystal of thought," the fusion of remote subtleties, the incorporeal ebb and flow of scruples and guilelessness—and these make up the perfect image of the waif ambitions and aspirations that dart and drift across a poet's downcast dreaming face.

PORTRAIT OF STÉPHANE MALLARMÉ, 1876. (10¼ × 13¼")
LOUVRE, PARIS.

AN IMPERSONAL SUBVERSION

How else are we to view Manet if not as a man of destiny called upon to preside over a metamorphosis of the arts which was not only inevitable but long overdue? By the time he came on the scene, in the mid-19th century, the foundations of a whole world had largely crumbled away; an era had come to a close and modern times lay ahead. Hitherto art had been the appanage of kings and princes; its mission had been to express an inordinate, unexceptionable majesty which, tyranically, unified men. But of the majestic nothing remained that an artisan could take any pride in serving. From now on the men of letters, the sculptors, the painters who had once been "artisans" were "artists" and had nothing else but their own personality to express; they were their own masters, their own sovereign. The ambiguous name of "artist" covered both a new-found dignity and a pretension difficult to justify. Isn't the artist all too often a mere artisan puffed up with conceit and ambition, drunk with his own sense of self-importance? Once he is free of every restraint, and need no longer defer to the dictates of all-powerful patrons, his pretensions are in danger of outstripping his talents.

In the confusion brought on by an almost overnight emancipation Manet appears as the symbol of all the conflicting inclinations a free man is torn between. In retrospect the actions of his life resemble the spinning of a compass needle thrown out of kilter. Those who came after him were free to choose. Manet had no choice but to make a clean break with the old order. He had strength enough to turn his back upon the past, but in doing so he somehow lost confidence in himself, failed to grasp the real trend of events, and let himself be entirely unstrung by the jeers of the public. We can hardly blame him for floundering a little at first. Later, too late perhaps, he tried to follow in the wake of Impressionism, but Impressionism was a pale affair beside that whirl of possibilities which, one after another, had danced through his imagination, only to leave him perplexed. Meeting as he did with one rebuff after another, how could he possibly have seen his way clear or stilled the tumult of resentment within him? His agony began afresh each time some wretched jury rejected one of his pictures and turned to joy when at last, in 1881, he was awarded the *hors concours* medal and then the Légion d'Honneur.

What is hard to make out is Manet's self-effacement, his moral timidity. In the preface to the catalogue of the exhibition he held in 1867 at his own expense, he addressed himself in the most diffident terms to the public that had so brazenly manhandled him. "Monsieur Manet," he wrote, "has never meant to protest. On the contrary, it is against him, to his great surprise, that the protesting has been done. Monsieur Manet has always recognized genuine talent wherever it is to be found, and has presumed neither to overthrow a long-standing form of painting nor to create a new one." Could anything be farther from the ways of the present day, now that aggressiveness and high-powered propaganda, calculated to dazzle and amaze, have got the upper hand?

As a matter of fact, Manet lagged behind his times in this respect. Romanticism set out to be provocative, while the parallel impact of Baudelaire's childish distress and childish joys was calculated to shock. Manet could have done as much, but a sustained effort in this direction wore him out and left him to suffer the inevitable rebuff in painful silence. What he yearned for was encouragement, official success. The reason for this rather pathetic desire? What else but the need to compensate for that cumbersome *hypertrophy of the ego* which is the artist's lot, and which sets him apart from the artisan. The artisan had remained anonymous, while it is the desire to achieve recognition

PORTRAIT OF THÉODORE DURET, 1868. (17 × 13¾")
MUSÉE DU PETIT-PALAIS, PARIS.

from his *peers*—not, as with the artisan, from his *employers*—that enables the artist to avoid the pitfalls of an overweening egoism. But what if the crowd, the public at large, is not composed of his peers and turns a deaf ear on what he has to say? Is he then condemned, irremediably, to swell up with that peculiarly empty, futile kind of pride we associate with certain Romantics?

PORTRAIT OF BAUDELAIRE'S MISTRESS, 1862. (35½ × 44½")
MUSEUM OF FINE ARTS, BUDAPEST.

Baudelaire wrote to Manet in June 1865: "I don't care a damn for the human race." And, confident of his friend's complicity, he added: "You realize of course, my dear Manet, that this is all strictly between ourselves." At about the same time, in a defiant letter to his mother, he wrote, characteristically: "I should like to stir up the whole human race against me; in universal hostility I see a kind of satisfaction that would console me for everything else."

Whatever the consolations Baudelaire sought, however, Manet could not share them. He was not the man to make light of the rest of the world. He was not conceited enough for that. He hung back, unable either to snap his fingers at others or to come to terms with them. In Manet there was none of those dark, eruptive forces, the curse of Baudelaire's life and at the same time the source of his withering irony; had Manet possessed these he might have asserted himself more forcibly. As it was, he steered a non-committal course. Beside Baudelaire's personality his own seems almost insignificant. Yet, though he bid for its approval, he stood head and shoulders above the crowd of his day, which never did homage to anything authentically great, and borne on by his modesty, by his impersonality, he in the end accomplished more than Baudelaire.

As far as painting went, Baudelaire swore by Delacroix and the twilight beauties of an art that by now had become pointless. It is true that he encouraged Manet's early efforts, but he had nothing to give him in the way of effective support or guidance. He seems to have urged him "to go Spanish," though for the painter himself this was only a passing phase, not to say a dead end. The only pictures he is known to have genuinely liked are those curious compositions, often very fine, that Manet made in Paris, generally from such Spanish models as he could find to pose for him. One of the best of these is *The Spanish Ballet*, in which he blended "what he saw" with a desire to achieve an exotic effect. Similar to these is *Baudelaire's Mistress*; here, on the basis of a brilliant simplification, Manet transposed the merely picturesque into a delicate fugue of lace and calico. Baudelaire was fond of such pictures, though probably he courted the younger man's admiration (Manet was eleven years his junior) more than he really admired his work. Manet came of a wealthy family, lent him money in times of need (at his death in 1867 he owed Manet 500 francs, which were paid by his mother, Madame Aupick) and generously rendered him various services in Paris while Baudelaire was away in Belgium.

Champion of an inspired, intensely personal art, a brilliant rather than a profound mind, Baudelaire had little to give Manet apart from the stimulus of friendship, the awareness of an inner world and the promise of secret riches for the man willing to go in quest of them. This was a gift precious enough in itself, but no doubt it only served to mystify Manet. Yet he must have taken to heart not only Baudelaire's fundamental maxim, to the effect that beauty is "always a little strange," but also this reflection of the poet's, which occurs in his review of the 1845 Salon: "The painter, the true painter to come, will be he who wrests from the contemporary scene its epic side and shows us, through line and color, how great and poetic we are in our cravats and patent-leather boots."

By 1860 *Concert at the Tuileries*—in which we see Baudelaire himself, mingling with the crowd—had met these specifications, but it is not likely that the poet thought very highly of the picture. Though he reverted many times to themes of contemporary life, the painter of *Olympia* somehow always eluded the formal laws his friend laid down. Manet only deferred to Baudelaire's theories in one respect: he valued imagination (though this was precisely what he lacked) above nature, and this pitted him squarely against the trend of his time.

THE SPANISH BALLET, 1862. (24×36″)
THE PHILLIPS COLLECTION, WASHINGTON.

Manet never raised his voice or sought to lord it over others. He suffered in silence and worked hard to get clear of what, for him, was a wasteland. Nothing and nobody could help him. In this venture his only guide was a kind of *impersonal* anguish. It was not the painter's anguish alone, for it had spread, though they did not realize it, to the scoffers and revilers as well, who *lay in wait* for the paintings which were so repulsive to them then, but which in time filled the yawning emptiness of their hollow souls.

Manet, on whom their repulsion fed, was the exact opposite of the man who is possessed by an *idée fixe*, a *personal* image constantly before him that he must continually renew and vary at all costs. The solutions Manet tested out were not solutions for himself alone. What inspired him as much as anything was the prospect, for him an act of grace, of entering a new world of forms which would deliver him, and with him *the others*, from the bondage, the monotony, the falsehood of art forms that had served their time.

CONCERT AT THE TUILERIES, 1860-1861. (30 × 46¾″)
BY COURTESY OF THE TRUSTEES, NATIONAL GALLERY, LONDON.

34

THE DESTRUCTION OF THE SUBJECT

NOTHING in Manet's bourgeois antecedents seemed to pre- destine him for art. His father wanted to see him study law, but the young man stubbornly held out against this and was finally allowed to enroll in the studio of Thomas Couture, an academic painter of the dreariest kind who had made a great name for himself at the 1847 Salon with a mammoth historical painting full of extravagant architectural details. This work—*The Roman Orgy*, still in the Louvre and persistently reproduced in each new edition of the Larousse—is nicely described in these words of Baudelaire, written in 1851: "They throw together a bunch of wretches, male and female, got up like so many butcherboys and washerwomen off on a binge, they ask these heroic figures to be good enough to keep their improvised leers going full tilt for the time required to complete the operation, and then they fondly imagine that they have rendered another tragic or colorful episode of ancient history." Baudelaire, in this instance, was speaking of a practice then greatly in vogue amongst photographers. But these elaborate pastries were nothing in comparison with Couture's *Orgy*, a finicking, supremely insipid piece of painting preening itself in all the vulgar ostentation of the "grand manner."

Manet, as might be expected, was ill at ease in Couture's studio. His fellow student there, Antonin Proust, has left us a vivid account of his reaction to Couture's methods.

"On Mondays," wrote Proust, "when the pose was set for the whole week, Manet invariably got into a tiff with the models. It was customary for them, as soon as they stood up on the table, to strike some ridiculous attitude.

◄   THE STREET SINGER, 1862. (42½ × 68¾")
ON LOAN TO THE MUSEUM OF FINE ARTS, BOSTON.

" 'Why the devil can't you be natural?' Manet used to exclaim. 'Is that the way you stand when you go to the grocer's to buy a bunch of radishes?'

"Finally he got hold of a model named Donato who, I believe, later became an actor in one of the boulevard theaters and, after that, a mesmerizer somewhere. Everything went fine to begin with. But it wasn't long before Donato, after spending a little time with the other models, was sticking his chest out with the best of them, bulging his muscles and taking heroic poses. Manet was heart-broken."

Further on, though getting away from Manet's basic attitude to these methods of teaching, Proust brings out the animosity that arose between pupil and teacher.

"One day he managed to get Gilbert, the model, to take up a simple pose, partially clothed. When Couture walked into the studio and saw that the model had his clothes on, he burst out angrily:

" 'Is Gilbert being paid to pose with his clothes on? Whose stupid idea is this?'

" 'Mine,' spoke up Manet.

" 'Poor dear boy! If you go on like this you'll never be anything but the Daumier of our time.' "

Alone with Proust, Manet shook his head:

" 'Daumier! I could do worse. After all, that's better than being the Coypel of our time.' "

These incidents show us Manet resisting—as young men are wont to do—what the past attempted to foist on him. But his individual attitude was the first sign of a fundamental change soon to come over all European painting. Hitherto held in representational service, it now began moving towards the autonomy it has enjoyed since Manet's time. From the moment the model's extravagant pose got on his nerves, the issue was no longer in doubt. What Manet insisted upon, uncompromisingly, was an end to rhetoric in painting. What he insisted upon was painting that should rise in utter freedom, in natural silence, painting for its own sake, a song for the eyes of interwoven forms and colors.

OYSTERS, 1862. ($14\frac{3}{4} \times 17\frac{7}{8}''$).
COLLECTION OF DR AND MRS DAVID M. LEVY, NEW YORK.

Before Manet painters had expressed themselves in a kind of time-honored rhetoric, symbolized by the model in his heroic pose with his chest thrust out. Not only Coypel and Couture but all painters had expressed themselves in that strain. In former times painting had been anything but autonomous; it had been in fact an integral part of a majestic *whole* set up to dazzle the masses by the powers-that-be.

There came a day, however, when this vast didactic structure —erected and renewed time and again in the form of castles, churches, palaces and works of art calculated to awe the masses and bend them beneath the yoke of authority—lost its power to sway. It fell to pieces, its message was shown up as mere grandiloquence, and the once obedient masses turned away in search of something else.

Manet turned away from the very first, and though not altogether sure of what he was about, he began recasting things into a new order, a new world of forms. This is noticeable in a painting in which his means, great though they were, were not yet great enough to ensure complete mastery. Yet it would be impossible to disrupt conventional harmonies to better effect than in this *Old Musician*, one of his first large-scale compositions. Notable above all for many fine details, it nevertheless successfully opposes a realistic, true-to-life ungainliness to Couture's hollow, architectural theatricality. Every part of the picture is wonderfully complete in itself; for example the sober simplicity—worthy of Watteau's *Gilles* —of the small boy in the straw hat, or the casually lounging figure of the old vagabond on the right, with his battered top hat. The models sit and stand more or less haphazardly, much as actors on stage taken unawares as they wait for the curtain to go up. And this, I think, is the effect Manet deliberately aimed at: not a carefully arranged pose, but a natural disorder arrived at by chance.

THE OLD MUSICIAN, 1862. (73¾ × 98″)
CHESTER DALE COLLECTION, NATIONAL GALLERY OF ART, WASHINGTON.

It was in the Batignolles district near his studio—"Little Poland," as it was then called, a ghetto-like quarter of Paris that passed away with the 19th century—that Manet found the people who posed for this picture, whose random lay-out contrasts with the forthright realism of the models.

PAGES 40-41: THE OLD MUSICIAN (DETAILS), 1862.
CHESTER DALE COLLECTION, NATIONAL GALLERY OF ART, WASHINGTON.

Reaction against the stale and conventional, which lies at the source of this disorder, is a recurrent phenomenon in the history of art (and in history in general). But we are prone to overlook the fact for the simple reason that, until recently, art history had been exclusively the history of the *fine* arts, of *beautiful* works of art, rarely if ever dealing with that fundamental divergence of outlook which opposes present-day art to that of the past.

Yet Baudelaire—no art historian, but a poet—was able to give a satisfactory account of this profound change, this reaction, of which his friend Manet's canvases were to be, in a few years' time, the most advanced expression.

"As you emerge from the exhibition," he suggested in his *Salon de 1846,* "compare the present age with past ages, or after visiting a newly decorated church, go rest your eyes in some museum of antiques, and analyse the differences.

"In the one: turbulence, a hubbub of styles and colors, a cacaphony of tones, overwhelming vulgarity, prosaic gestures and attitudes, sham nobility, every known variety of stereotype, and all this plain to see, not only in pictures placed side by side, but in one and the same picture; in short, a complete absence of unity, which only produces eyestrain and a frightful headache.

"In the other, that sense of respect which comes over us, which touches us to the quick, is the effect not of the yellow varnish and the ravages of time, but of an underlying unity. For a great Venetian painting clashes less with a Giulio Romano than some of our paintings—and not the worst of the lot— do with each other when placed side by side."

Baudelaire saw that in his time the old forms had been sundered. In his eyes the former "schools" of painting were proof of a monumental order of things, and the guarantee of unity and lasting tradition. "There were still schools under

Louis XV," he wrote, "and still one in the days of the Empire —one school, in other words the impossibility of any disagreement or doubt... Doubt, or the absence of faith and naïveté, is a vice peculiar to this century. Today no one obeys. And naïveté, which is the ascendancy of temperament over breeding, is a divine privilege withheld from nearly all of us."

No doubt Baudelaire only vaguely grasped the connection between the decline underway in his time—obvious to him —and the majestic forms which had imposed themselves on society with such success in the past. Still he put his finger on the secret of that success: the presence behind those forms of an all-powerful element of compulsion and authority exercised on the masses from above, to which they bowed in collective submission. "Few men," he went on, "have the right to rule, for few men are moved by a great passion." And further on: "The present state of painting is the result of an anarchic freedom which glorifies the individual, however puny he may be."

This is a picture of a world familiar to us all. Nevertheless, it may be well to look more closely into its meaning. First of all, the meaning Baudelaire elicited in the world of his day:

"Anyone today who has to be classed among the imitators, even among the more clever ones, is and will always be no more than a second-rate painter. In the past he might have made an excellent artisan. Today he's a dead loss both for himself and for us.

"For this reason it might have been better, for the sake of their welfare and even their personal happiness, had the half-hearted been exposed to the hickory-stick of an exacting faith; for the strong are few, and today it would take Delacroix or Ingres to keep afloat in the chaos of a sterile, all-consuming freedom."

But Ingres and Delacroix were no more than relics of the past in the midst of the "decline." They had nothing new to

STILL LIFE WITH MELON AND PEACHES, CA. 1866. (27 × 36¼″)
BY COURTESY OF MR AND MRS EUGENE MEYER, WASHINGTON.

offer. Their painting is like that of the past in that it merely
filled its appointed part in a system of rhetoric. Delacroix
bluffly stood up and declaimed rather than spoke his part,
while Ingres—I think we can grant him this—at least acted with
a certain discretion that links him up with what came afterwards. Delacroix, it is fair to add, availed himself with some

reluctance of the architectural order handed down to him, which the weltering tumult of his own forms, instead of rounding out or completing, only disrupted. Anyhow there was nothing in the painting of either to meet the problem raised by the now irrevocable disappearance of any majestic governing influence, nothing that could have dominated the vulgar agitation of the crowd.

This is about as far as Baudelaire's critical insight seems to have carried. There is not a great deal to be said for the vision implied in the principle he recommended to the painters of his time: to throw convention to the winds and represent contemporary figures in contemporary dress. This does not go far enough.

Baudelaire was apparently fond of Manet's early work, but from the time he left Paris (1864) until his death (in 1867, two years after *Olympia* was shown at the Salon) he wrote nothing about his friend's work. Nothing but the letter from Brussels, which Manet received while miserably depressed over the *Olympia* scandal. Comparing the sneers that greeted *Olympia* with those that greeted Chateaubriand, Delacroix and Wagner, he gave Manet a friendly scolding. After all, he said, "you are only the first in the decline of your art." This amounts to saying that he approved of Manet's art without grasping the meaning of its "individual" vigor, which, in his eyes, resisted the "decline" then in progress but still belonged to that "hubbub of styles and colors" which—except for Ingres and Delacroix, and also Courbet and Corot—characterized the painting of his time.

PAGE 46: VICTORINE MEUREND IN THE COSTUME OF AN ESPADA, 1862. (65 × 50¼″) COURTESY OF THE METROPOLITAN MUSEUM OF ART, NEW YORK.

PAGE 47: TORERO SALUTING, 1866. (67⅜ × 44½″) COURTESY OF THE METROPOLITAN MUSEUM OF ART, NEW YORK.

46

ANGELINA, 1865. (35¾ × 28¼″)
MUSÉE DU LUXEMBOURG, PARIS.

What Baudelaire failed to see is that, by breaking with the past, Manet elicited from this decline a compensation denied both Ingres and Delacroix, and denied Courbet too (Corot standing aloof in this respect). The breakdown of rhetorical painting was opening the way to a new form of painting, one familiar to us today but undreamed-of then and achieved by Manet alone—by the painter who preferred his models to pose haphazardly, in disorder.

In *Saturne*, his study of Goya, Malraux has this to say: "Goya foreshadows Manet, Daumier and one side of Cézanne. To prepare the way for the latter, art had to be purged of the metaphysical passion that ravaged Goya; it had to become *an end in itself* [my italics]. In some of Goya's last portraits, in some of his last canvases, it became just this. The man for whom dream was half and perhaps the more important half of life, delivered painting from the dream-life. With Goya painting gained the right to look at reality no longer as mere raw material... and to transform it into that specific world musicians know so well."

I cannot say whether it is correct to attribute this achievement to Goya, whose paintings were never till today beheld in the light Malraux sees them in. Deaf, wrapped up in himself, Goya brought little influence to bear. He dominates the painting of the last two centuries, but only recently have we become aware of that silent prompting which led him to paint some of his most powerful works, for himself alone, on the walls of what his neighbors called the "Deaf Man's House." In a sense, Goya made no effort to communicate, but in his deafness lived out his own dream, having stoically abandoned all hope of making himself heard.

The silence of his world is above all the silence born of an outcry, a desperate attempt to express the *impossible*.

Nevertheless, all his paintings, drawings and etchings told something, conveyed a meaning. Except for a few rare works, they were never reduced to the pure play of colors and forms.

In others besides Manet we can discern the transition from narrative, anecdotal painting to pure painting—"patches, colors, movement." Malraux lists a certain number of names. Unmistakable hints appear in the work of Chardin, Delacroix, Courbet, Turner—in painting generally perhaps.

But Manet was the first to practise the art of painting taken for itself alone, what we call today "modern painting." Manet's *Execution of Maximilian*, writes Malraux, "is Goya's *Shootings of May Third* minus what the latter picture signifies." With Manet began the repudiation of "all values foreign to painting," the indifference to the meaning of the subject. Malraux stresses the decisive part played by Manet when he says: "A washerwoman by Manet is like one by Daumier minus what the latter picture signifies." And more explicitly: "The moderns stand apart [from Daumier] by their repudiation of all values foreign to painting."

Yet, in a sense, Malraux is right in connecting Goya with the birth of modern art. During his stay in Spain Manet took little interest in Goya. For him the great thing at the Prado was Velazquez, who stood closest to pure painting. Though on the whole his art belongs to the past, Goya made a frantic effort to wrench free of those bonds. His means, to be sure, resemble those that went to build and decorate the temple of the past, but straining his forces to the limit he undermined the temple's foundations. Out of step with his times, he did violence to everything that structure stood for. It was meant to shield, to reassure, to asseverate. From inside it Goya cried out the temple's incapacity to give him peace; he broadcast the absurdity, the lunatic cruelty, the rottenness of the whole structure. Goya came as a thief in the night to burn the temple;

he was the fierce negative product of academicism, whose positive side was mere death—emptiness, decline and death.

Goya, we may say, was a storm which, when occasionally it subsided, gave a glimpse of the immense possibilities of the new age that would follow the downfall of the old. Malraux rightly points to *The Milkmaid of Bordeaux* as no more than a pure play of light, flickering beneath the old painter's hand. Thirty years earlier the frescos in the church of San Antonio de la Florida at Madrid had expressed much the same thing. The grandeur of both no doubt sprang from the storm raging within him—a grandeur whose elements were grouping themselves anew, having survived a past out of which Goya, stifling in its toils, drew the most incendiary visions ever recorded in paints.

In that vision of a man about to die, flinging up his arms with a shriek, which we call *The Shootings of May Third*, we have the very image of death, such as man can hardly ever know it, since the event itself wipes out all consciousness of it. In this picture Goya caught the blinding, instantaneous flash of death, a thunderbolt of sight-destroying intensity, brighter than any known light. The eloquence, the rhetoric of painting has never been carried further, but here its effect is that of definitive silence, an outcry smothered before it can rise.

Manet saw this painting at Madrid in 1865 and in 1867 painted *The Execution of Maximilian*.

These two famous pictures invite comparison. They are not unrelated, but the difference between them is striking. Manet deliberately rendered the condemned man's death with the same indifference as if he had chosen a fish or a flower for his subject. True, the picture relates an incident, no less than Goya's does, but—and this is what counts—without the least concern for the incident itself. Many other pictures by the painter of *The Balcony* have nothing to relate, no extra-pictorial message to convey, but *The Execution of Maximilian* is the most tight-lipped of them all. In it Manet paid scrupulous attention to detail, but even this is negative, and the picture as a whole is the negation of eloquence; it is the negation of that kind of painting which, like language, expresses sentiments and relates anecdotes.

Thereafter, Malraux feels, Manet never quite shook off the effect of this picture. Though *Maximilian* is not one of those rare paintings in which Manet arrived at the inaccessible, it seems to me that in it he overcame the difficulty he tackled. Malraux admits as much: here Manet wrung the last drop of meaning out of the subject. To suppress and destroy the subject is exactly what modern painting does, but this does not mean that the subject is altogether absent. To some extent every picture has its subject, its title, but now these have shrunk to insignificance; they are mere *pretexts* for the painting itself. On the face of it, death, coldly, methodically dealt out by a firing-squad, precludes an indifferent treatment; such a subject is nothing if not charged with meaning for each one of us. But Manet approached it with an almost callous indifference that the spectator, surprisingly enough, shares to the full. *Maximilian* reminds us of a tooth deadened by novocain; we get the impression of an all-engulfing numbness, as if a skillful practitioner had radically cured painting of a centuries-old ailment: chronic eloquence. Manet posed some of his models in the attitude of dying, some in the attitude of killing, but all more or less casually, as if they were about to "buy a bunch of radishes." Every strain of eloquence, feigned or genuine, is done away with. There remain a variety of color patches and the impression that the subject ought to have induced an emotional reaction but has failed to do so—the curious impression of an absence.

The death sentence passed in a far-off land on this Habsburg prince—whom the reckless ambitions of the French emperor Napoleon III had inveigled into a hare-brained scheme for the conquest of Mexico—came as a shock to the "civilized" world. No one imagined that the execution would really be carried out, but the Mexicans disregarded the concert of protest raised by many nations and Maximilian courageously met his death on June 19, 1867. Hardly had the news been received in France than Manet painted this large canvas, which the French government sternly forbade him to exhibit.

THE EXECUTION OF THE EMPEROR MAXIMILIAN, 1867. (79¼ × 119¾″)
KUNSTHALLE, MANNHEIM.

54

It may be argued that somehow this picture does not "come off," that these color patches fail to "sing." This very absence of effect, however, gives rise to an imponderable plenitude which, once perceived, is completely satisfying. This quality is not to be found in eloquent painting, however sober, in Meissonier's for example, a contemporary of Manet. This imponderable plenitude is perhaps essential to what modern man really is, supremely, silently, when he consents to reject the pompous rhetoric that seems to give sense to every-day life, but which actually falsifies our feelings and commits them to a ludicrous abjection. *The Execution of Maximilian*—negatively speaking—represents a full world, free of the insipid comedies, the dust and litter of the past. And despite the contrast between this picture and *The Shootings of May Third*, there is one striking similarity: in both, painting accedes to "definitive silence." *Maximilian* accedes to it in the suppression of "all values foreign to painting."

The importance of this similarity must not be minimized. It is a curious fact that something in Manet's character led him from time to time to represent death in his painting. We have *The Dead Toreador*, in which the position of the body is copied from Velazquez; the same position recurs in a drawing of a dead body lying in the street, which he made during the Paris Commune. At the same time he reverted to the theme of *The Execution of Maximilian*, using it for street scenes he observed and wished to record. *The Funeral*, dating from early 1870, again betrays the attraction exerted on him by the idea of death. But in *The Suicide* (1877), with the pistol still clutched in a limply hanging hand, we have the clearest demonstration of his desire to subordinate—or sublimate—the horror of death in a naïvely unconcerned play of light.

◄   THE FIFER, 1866. (62¾ × 38½″) LOUVRE, PARIS.

Modern painting attains through *absence* what Goya, in a world freighted with solemnity and grave respect, attained through *excess*. A stranger to it, Manet was *absent* from that gravity which Goya transformed into excess, carrying it to an unendurable pitch. Goya's world sometimes partakes of the sacred, but it surges up out of remote, primitive depths; then it violently disowns the solemn conventions of the day. Our modern art—clean-cut through silence and the elimination of conventional sentiments—is, on the other hand, fashioned round a core of inner, underlying violence. For all the dark and dreary forces around him, Goya achieved something of this clean-cut clarity by going those forces one better. Thus in a sense he was the first of the moderns, though Manet alone explicitly inaugurated modern painting.

We are often led astray by the complexity of the human forms involved in the rise of modern art. That complexity, however, is reducible to its simplest elements.

In the past art was the expression of "supreme" forms, divine and royal (one and the same thing in early times). Though adulterated and pratically meaningless by Manet's time, they yet lingered on. The triumph of the bourgeoisie—incapable of conceiving anything truly majestic that might compel and command unconditionally—hastened their disintegration. The upshot was an anarchy of forms, fraught with possibilities, but saddled still with the last remnants of majestic forms, even though no one could possibly believe in them any longer.

The majestic forms of old had drawn their strength from the people's naïveté, which was now lost to them. Christianity lived on, but Christian naïveté was no longer a living force. The aristocracy, in such a situation, no longer had any role to play; having lost its naïveté, it had become bourgeois.

The people by itself cannot create new forms. The bourgeoisie of the 19th century, which alone had the leisure to create them, had split up into partisans of an empty tradition and detractors of that tradition. The latter, however, while denying that tradition in art, did not deny it in politics. ("Strange," said Manet, himself a republican, "how republicans turn into reactionaries the minute they speak about art.") As a matter of fact what they really rejected were not the forms as they had been in their prime, but the pale shadow of them which had survived. Thus Manet rejected Couture, but not Titian and Rembrandt. The other artists who did not make this distinction, but continued to pay homage to a false majesty, were simply debasing themselves. What had to be found, above and beyond conventional majestic forms, was some supreme, unimpeachable reality capable of withstanding the immense pressure of a utilitarian tradition.

THE DEAD TOREADOR, 1864. (29¾ × 60½″)
JOSEPH WIDENER COLLECTION, NATIONAL GALLERY OF ART, WASHINGTON.

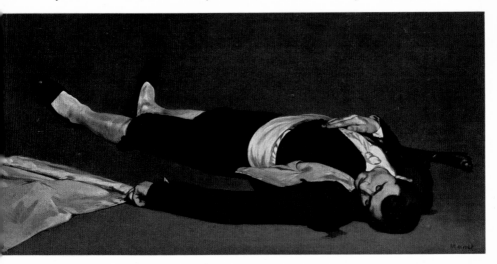

This supreme reality was found in the silence of art. What is supreme and majestic in present-day life is not to be found in present-day forms, which are incapable of giving rise to palaces and temples; it resides in that "secret royalty" which Malraux reads into Cézanne's apples, which made its appearance in *Olympia*, and which is the greatness of *The Execution of Maximilian*. This royalty springs not from any given image, but from the passion of the painter who, within himself, fathoms the depths of supreme silence, in which his painting is transfigured and which in turn it expresses. After this, painting becomes the art of wresting objects, and the images of objects, from a world that has surrendered to a bourgeois torpor.

André Malraux was the first to state it clearly: the only cathedral raised in our time is the vast collection of modern paintings in our museums. But it is essentially a secret cathedral. That which is sacred today can no longer be advertised; from now on, what is sacred is mute. Our modern world can only experience an inner transfiguration, silent and in a sense negative. To speak of it, as I have done, is to speak of a definitive silence.

I might add that, in our museums, with modern painting hung beside that of the past, the latter enters into a comparable silence. It does so as soon as it is removed from its original context; out of that context its original message loses its meaning. So it is that, for us today, the beauty of the Old Masters' art is similar in kind to that of modern painting, since we no longer have eyes or ears for the message that was once attached to it. We see something else today, we see that magic interplay of light that lies above or beneath the literal significance of the forms. What we perceive today in these majestic images is not the expression of a well-defined majesty, bound up with political or mythological constructions, but the expression of a majesty quite devoid of political implications. This simpler, unassuming majesty is that of every genuinely free man; it is the limitless interplay of all possible forms. But in this kinship of the painting of all periods, Goya's art has a place apart; the very silence it attains brings it nearer to us. Goya, though a party to the system he was undermining, deliberately looked to art as the supreme value—to art and to the silence in which he gritted his teeth.

Generally speaking, the more our outlook is governed by the decrepit system of the past as it continues to act upon us like a habit that will not be shaken off, the less inclined we are to assign a supreme value to art. It is not easy for us to attribute to the familiar world of the here-and-now, in which today art is created and disseminated, the power once reserved for a sphere far transcending the ordinary mortal. Nevertheless art once depended on this transcendence for its very being—pending the day when a strange, unaccountable agitation came over it. Then, out of the confusion, a whole new milieu came into being, born of the daily contacts of painters and poets, a milieu with all the curious and exaggerated features of a sect, but without its ready-made pretexts for coming into existence. True, these contacts and the passionate intensity behind them were only to be found in 19th-century France, for it was there that skepticism went deepest, and there that evidence of the collapse of the past was most tangible.

THE OLYMPIA SCANDAL

IT was also in France that the public openly declared war on the new art, and this with a spleen and exasperation that rapidly assumed alarming proportions.

It is only natural for an innovation to meet with resistance, especially from those only superficially attached—by force of habit rather than conviction—to the forms of the past. They resist it all the more fiercely if that innovation goes deep enough to threaten the foundations of a familiar order of things. Past ages, confident in the supreme value of their ideals and achievements, could afford to look tolerantly on the changes that came with passing time. The Parisian public, on the other hand, rose up in arms against Manet not in a moment of aberration, but because it lucidly realized that his painting profaned everything it had been taught to believe in. But Manet stood firm, determined to see the struggle through at all costs. "From Baudelaire to Verlaine, from Daumier to Modigliani, what a toll of human sacrifice! Seldom have so many great artists offered up so many sacrifices to an unknown god. Unknown, since those who served him, though they felt his grandeur, recognized it nowhere but in their own form of expression—painting" (Malraux). Unknown he may have been, but once a breach had been made in the old order through the agency of painting, it was clearly felt, at least by the sentient few, that the reign of the new god had begun.

A conflict had divided the bourgeoisie against itself. Though the aristocracy had lost its vital energy, bourgeois conformism blindly clung to the empty forms of that vitality. Opposed to the conformist bourgeoisie stood a handful of non-conformist artists. The conflict between the two broke out with a vengeance at the 1865 Salon, where *Olympia* was exhibited.

Olympia is generally regarded as Manet's masterpiece, and I share this view. It was also the picture that at last unleashed the full fury of the public, which, as if led by some unerring instinct to the lair of danger, seemed momentarily endowed with the gift of insight.

We have seen how essential the *destruction of the subject*— at least of the meaning it conveyed—was to *The Execution of Maximilian*. It was even more essential to *Olympia*. But before we pursue this point, a few quotations from the Parisian press of that day will give a graphic idea of the clamor that went up at sight of this painting.

Such a picture might "stir up a revolt," protested one Jean Ravenel in *L'Epoque*. And Jules Claretie in *L'Artiste:* "What on earth is this yellow-bellied odalisque, this wretched model picked up God knows where and pawned off as representing Olympia?" Ernest Chesneau, a critic who later stood up for Manet, wrote in *Le Constitutionnel:* "He manages to provoke a good deal of shameless snickering, which causes crowds to gather in front of this ludicrous creature he calls Olympia." The daughter of Théophile Gautier wrote in *L'Entr'acte:* "The exhibition has its clown. Among all the artists is one who turns somersaults and sticks out his tongue." "Never has there been a spectacle to equal it or anything quite so cynical as this Olympia, a kind of female gorilla," exclaimed Amédée Cantaloube in *Le Grand Journal.* In *Le Petit Journal* Edmond About tried to sum things up: "Peace to Monsieur Manet! Public ridicule has done justice to his pictures." The deepest shudder of all ran through Paul de Saint-Victor, a senior critic whose opinions carried weight: "The crowd gathers round Monsieur Manet's highly spiced *Olympia* as it would round a body at the morgue. Art that has sunk so low is not worthy of our censure. 'Speak not of them, only gaze and pass on,' says Virgil to Dante as they make their way across one of the circles of hell."

Such were the critical fireworks that went up when one of the present-day masterpieces of the Louvre was first exhibited.

It is interesting to note the attitude of Théophile Gautier, the poet Baudelaire esteemed so highly. He had loudly applauded Manet's early efforts, and even before that, in 1830, in the uproar over Victor Hugo's play *Hernani*, had proudly sported the crimson waistcoat that then symbolized the sworn enemies of bourgeois conformism. But how did he see *Olympia*?

"In the opinion of many it is enough to move on and laugh; this is a mistake. Monsieur Manet is not so easily dismissed. He has a school, a following, even fanatical admirers; his influence reaches farther than might be supposed. Monsieur Manet has the distinction of being a menace. But all danger is now past. *Olympia* cannot be explained from any point of view, not even by taking it for what it is: a languid model stretched out on a sheet. Flesh-tints are dingy, modeling inexistent. Shadows are indicated by streaks of tan of varying width. What to make of the colored woman holding a bouquet wrapped in paper and the black cat tracking dirt over the bed? We could still forgive the ugliness of it all, were it true, studied, relieved by some splendid effect of color. Here, we are sorry to say, there is nothing but the desire to catch the eye at any price."

Several years later (in *Le Moniteur* of May 11, 1868) another article by Gautier shows, nevertheless, how keenly aware he was of the change coming over the times.

"Each of us, though no one admits it, is apparently afraid of being taken for a Philistine, a bourgeois, a hopeless fool with a fondness for drawing-room miniatures and copies painted on china, or worse yet old-fashioned enough to find something commendable in David's *Rape of the Sabine Women*. One takes stock of oneself almost in terror, wondering if one has not grown fat and bald, and incapable of following the bold flights of youth...

"Everyone wonders: 'Am I really an old fogey, a prehistoric fossil?' One recalls the shudders of horror, thirty years ago, aroused by the first paintings of Delacroix, Decamps, Boulanger, Corot, Rousseau, banished for so long from the Salon. Ingres himself had great difficulty in getting accepted. He was accused of taking art back to the grotesque barbarity of the 16th century. The phrase comes straight from an article of the period. Confronted by these novelties, the serious-minded could only wonder whether it is possible to understand anything in art but the works of the generation of one's youth. Very probably the pictures of Courbet, Manet, Monet and others like them contain beauties which we long-haired romantics overlook.

"Does this amount to saying, then, that for us there is absolutely nothing in Monsieur Manet's painting? He has a quality that gives a distinctive style to his every canvas: the absolute unity of local tones. But it must be added that this is obtained only at the expense of modeling, chiaroscuro, transition passages and detail."

Possibly, as Gautier ruefully suggests, our ability to appreciate art is fixed for good, indeed arrested, by "the bold flights of our youth." But this view implies a gradual, regular evolution comparable to vegetable growth, a quantitative difference, as it were, being steadily registered with each succeeding generation. The law of progress Gautier lays down could only make sense if it had always held good in the past and went on holding good in the future. The truth is that it hardly came into play at all before Gautier's time. As for the present-day, it seems safe to say that, at least since 1930, there has been nothing new or bold enough to draw a sharp dividing-line between the elder and the younger generation. The intellectual movements reflected in painting may well be clearer and more obvious, if not more profound, than those reflected in other arts. From Impressionism, insofar as it began with Manet, up to Surrealism, by way of Fauvism and Cubism, a violent upheaval occurred; painting was racked by a prolonged fever, punctuated by periodic outbursts of public indignation. No one can claim to define them precisely, but these various movements, it seems to me, were only successive phases of one vast change. This change was not the transition from one well-defined state to another. After all, the distance separating Meissonier (whom Delacroix admired) from *Olympia* is no less vast than that separating Meissonier from Picasso. It is the same distance; the only difference is that after Manet it was more and more forcibly stressed—and by an impressive array of very great painters. In the past twenty or twenty-five years, however, no one has come up with a new way of stressing it.

The present monograph is not the place to speculate on the significance of this situation for us today; in any case it is too early yet to see clearly ahead. The various kinds of painting that have arisen since Manet's time represent the varied possibilities of painting in this new realm we have entered, where silence reigns profoundly and art is the supreme value—art *in general*, which means man as an individual, self-sustaining, detached from any collective enterprise or prescribed system (and also from individualism). Here the work of art takes the place of everything that in the past—even in the remotest past— was sacred and majestic.

We enter this new realm as the curtain goes up on

"OLYMPIA"

Elle dégage une horreur sacrée.
Elle est scandale, idole...
Sa tête est vide: un fil de velours noir l'isole
de l'essentiel de son être...

Manet 23

OLYMPIA, 1863. ($51 \times 74\frac{3}{4}"$) LOUVRE, PARIS.

Manet's most famous picture owed its initial notoriety to the terrific outcry that went up when it was first exhibited publicly at the 1865 Salon. Not even Picasso's most startling canvases can claim to have excited a comparable reaction. Yet we cannot help wondering what further heights might have been reached by the passions of the crowd, had they been able to foresee that 40 years later, in 1907, the object of their deprecation would take its place in the Louvre? Indignation and admiration—these two reactions to *Olympia*, before and after, are perhaps the most significant characteristic of the art history of our time. What first incensed the multitude has repeatedly proved to be an authentic renewal of beauty. As time passes, however, it becomes increasingly difficult for us to find anything shocking in modern works of art, since the initial element of scandal presupposed some barrier of convention that has now been effectively torn down.

Paul Valéry—from whom I take these verses, lifting them from a context that does not concern us here—also associates *Olympia* with a line from Baudelaire originally written as a tribute to another painting by Manet. But it is certainly *Olympia*, not *Lola de Valence*, in which we see the scintillation of

Le charme inattendu d'un bijou rose et noir...

Valéry detected "a true affinity of inquietudes" between Baudelaire and Manet. But the parallel he drew is only superficial. "We need only skim through the slender volume of *Les Fleurs du Mal*," he wrote, "note the significant, well-consolidated diversity of subject-matter in those poems, and compare it with the diversity of themes that stands out in the catalogue of Manet's works"—adding: "The man who wrote *Bénédiction, Tableaux Parisiens, Bijoux* and *Vin des Chiffonniers* must somehow be deeply related to the man who successively painted *Christ with Angels, Olympia, Lola de Valence* and *The Absinthe Drinker*." Even were the similarity of subject-matter greater still, this would not be sufficient ground for linking painter and poet so closely. These premises led Valéry to a very dubious interpretation of *Olympia*. "Cold, naked Olympia, trite monster of love, flattered by a Negro woman," is in his eyes "one of Society's most ignoble arcana raised to power and held up to the public gaze." She is "woman pre-eminently unclean, she whose status requires guileless ignorance of all decency. Bestial vestal dedicated to absolute nakedness, she sets the mind musing on all the primitive barbarity and ritual animality lurking and sustained in the ways and workings of big-city prostitution."

It is possible (but debatable) that something of this was the initial *text* of *Olympia*. But text and painting part company, just as *The Execution of Maximilian* parts company with the newspaper account of the tragic events at Queretaro. In both cases the picture *obliterates* the text, *and the meaning of the picture is not in the text behind it but in the obliteration of that text*. *Olympia* is meaningful only to the extent that Manet was unwilling to say what Valéry said, to the extent, on the contrary, that Manet flushed out of the picture the literal sense Valéry read into it. In her provocative literalness she is nothing. Her real nudity (not merely that of her body) is the silence that emanates from her, like that from a sunken ship. All we have is the "sacred horror" of her presence—presence whose sheer simplicity is tantamount to absence. Her harsh realism—which, for the Salon public, was no more than a gorilla-like ugliness—is inseparable from the concern Manet had to reduce *what he saw* to the mute and utter simplicity of *what was there*. Zola's realism *located* what it described; Manet departed from realism by virtue of the power he had—at least in *Olympia*—of not locating his subject *anywhere*, neither in the drab world of naturalistic prose nor in that, typified by Couture, of absurd academic fictions. The latter, to judge from *Olympia*, might never have existed.

What shocked was the ruthlessness with which Manet wiped the slate clean, and also the starkness—which charms us today—of an art converted into the supreme value (or the supreme charm) and not into the majesty of conventional sentiments, which once made the grandeur of reigning princes. We admire this straightforward humanity that says what it has to say regardless of the conventional standards governing eloquent expression, whether in written, spoken or pictorial form. Looking at *Olympia*, we feel very keenly that something has been suppressed; we feel a charm refined to its purest—a pure state of being, sovereignly, silently cut off from the old lies set up in the name of eloquence.

From now on, outwardly at least, the break was complete and plain to see. In Manet's borrowings, however, we have an interesting sidelight on his methods. A number of times he took over the lay-out of an old print or painting. It is common knowledge that *Le Déjeuner sur l'herbe* was patterned on Raphael's *Judgment of Paris* as engraved by Marcantonio. The lay-out of *Olympia* was derived from Titian's *Urbino Venus*, which Manet copied at the Uffizi in Florence in 1856. In both he took a mythological theme and transposed it into the world of his day. This metamorphosis is already hinted at in the 1856 copy, which is much closer to us than the original is, containing none of the unreal sweetness of the "divine" figure Titian represented. Even then Manet's rash, impassioned manner

THE URBINO VENUS (COPY AFTER TITIAN), 1856. (9½ × 14½")
PRIVATE COLLECTION, PARIS.

brought the goddess down to earth and inflicted human standards on her. But this copy gave only the faintest hint of the change to come. Only with *Olympia* do we reach that *moulting time*, when painting cast off its old trappings and emerged as a new reality.

All of a sudden the divine figure burst from the mists in which, unaffected by the human condition, the majesty and beauty of superhuman forms had once towered so high. She awoke with a start to the everyday world. *Venus* was heavy with languor; *Olympia* sits up and asserts her presence, raising her head, shifting her elbow, gazing straight at us like the pert and very real young woman she is. The setting is virtually intact: the partition on the left dividing the background in two, the drape in the upper lefthand corner. The maid-servant, however, has lost all resemblance with that of Titian's *Venus*; she faces us now, standing beside her mistress's couch, the milky pink of her dress contrasting sharply with her features, for she is now a colored woman. The dog, which in Titian lay curled up at the foot of the bed, has got to its feet and been changed by Manet into a black cat. Though unimportant in themselves, these changes are the outward signs of the transition from one world to another. The world of mythology was nothing without the dignity which, forthwith, assimilated it to the world of theology, of which it was only an elegant variant, devoid of tragic import, but still imbued with poetic majesty.

Unimportant changes, but they brought Manet face to face with a problem that had once seemed insoluble: how is the artist to treat the prosaic aspects of contemporary man? When Houdon made his statue of Voltaire, he draped him in a Roman toga, and was no doubt right in doing so. At about the same time Diderot wrote as follows in his *Pensées détachées sur la peinture:* "When a nation is shabbily dressed, its costume had best be left alone." From Antonin Proust we learn that Manet came across this passage and, though hardly more than a boy at the time, reacted to it at once. "But that's sheer nonsense," he said to Proust. "An artist has got to move with his times and paint what he sees." Manet did just that; from the very start, at Couture's studio, he would have none of models who struck heroic poses, but agreed wholeheartedly with Baudelaire —"How great and poetic we are in our cravats and patent-leather boots." The true painter sees as much and makes others see it. *Concert at the Tuileries* (in which we see Baudelaire himself in a top hat) puts this principle into practice. Painted in 1860 or 1861 and exhibited in March 1863 at the Galerie Martinet, this picture signalized the outbreak of the "Manet scandal." Other canvases there (Manet exhibited fourteen) might have incensed the public, but Tabarant writes that "visitors took particular offense at *Concert at the Tuileries*." "One exasperated art-lover," Zola later said, "went so far as to threaten to take matters into his own hands if *Concert at the Tuileries* were not promptly removed from the gallery." This gentleman's indignation undoubtedly sprang from the conviction, stronger during the Second Empire than in the 18th century when Diderot was writing, that to show people in everyday dress was an outrage against art. (Oddly enough, Baudelaire, entirely absorbed by Manet's "Spanish" paintings, never mentioned this picture, which answered his prescriptions perfectly.)

I may have seemed to minimize the *Olympia* scandal by reducing it to the transition from outworn art forms to those of modern life. Not at all; everything that incensed the public in *Olympia* had already appeared in *Concert at the Tuileries*, though in different form. *Olympia*, obviously, is a young woman stark naked, whereas the gentlemen in the *Tuileries* are dressed in black frock-coats and have "something somber and supernatural on their heads" (as Mallarmé wittily described their top hats).

But after all *Olympia* is a woman and not a goddess; she and the men in frock-coats live in the same world—a world art obstinately sought to ignore. Painting, as I have said, had represented the majestic forms of the past, which it had done, at least to some degree, within the setting of the real world; for painting was then expected to *represent*—it could not *create*. This being so, Manet's point of view—that "an artist has got to move with the times and paint what he sees"—amounted to blasphemy. What was the art of the past if not "that gigantic theological poem" of Marcel Proust whose function was to impose silence on everything else? Whether theological, mythological or simply dynastic, this poem was always the expression of a truth transcending the earthbound, transcending *what we see*. *Olympia* burst naked—but a woman, not a goddess—from that world, which had its charms, poetic as far as it went, but conventional through and through.

Poetry, in the past, endeavored to be real, but to do so had to reduce itself to a convention which alone ventured to read the strange stuff of poetry into the reality of things. Where the convention was missing, it was furiously denied that any poetry existed. But what is poetry but a vehement negation of all convention? It is utterly simple and unassuming, unreal and unattached, drawing its *magic* from within itself, not from the structure of a world whose political organization answered to the dream of a majestic prince or divinity. Like modern poetry, *Olympia* is the negation of that world; it is the negation of mythological Olympus and everything it stood for.

In the same way, *Le Déjeuner sur l'herbe* is the negation of the *Concert champêtre*, in which Giorgione, though putting two nude women in the company of two musicians dressed in Renaissance costume, had done so on the strength of a Greek fable. Manet took over only the theme of the Louvre painting (he took the actual lay-out of his picture from a print), but, ignoring their mythological origin, he set both theme and lay-out in a contemporary context. By doing so, he deliberately broke with the past and laid the foundations of a new order. The nude woman of the *Déjeuner* sits beside two fully dressed men. The aim he set himself in his youth was realized here and in *Olympia*, which recapture the majesty of art, but in the immediate present, in the forms of modern times, all eloquence reduced to silence.

Manet might have foreseen the shock this was bound to produce on a convention-ridden public. In any event, he was only partially satisfied with *Le Déjeuner sur l'herbe*. The charm of the picture is undeniable, as are its forthright execution, its breadth and mastery, as well as what an anonymous writer in the *Gazette de France*—when it was first exhibited at the Salon des Refusés in 1863—called "this acid coloring" that "pierces the eye like a steel sawblade." (Rumors at the time attributed the article, or at least the views it expressed, to Delacroix. "Monsieur Manet," the anonymous critic went on, "has all the qualities needed to be unanimously rejected by every jury on earth... His figures stand out very sharply, with unrelieved, uncompromising harshness. He has all the bitterness of those green fruits that are destined never to ripen." Shortly after this Delacroix died, and the writer of the article, if not Delacroix himself, must have died about the same time, for this authoritative voice, hostile but sincere, was never heard again.) Manet's "acid coloring" was of course deliberate. But it is clear that he was not completely sure of himself in this picture, which was but one step in the systematic inquiry that led from *Concert at the Tuileries* to *Olympia*.

Antonin Proust records a remark by Manet that seems to have been the point of departure for *Le Déjeuner sur l'herbe*. In August 1862, on the Seine banks at Gennevilliers (which is known to have been the landscape setting of the picture), Manet

Manet 25

was watching some women bathers come out of the water when he turned to Proust and said: "It seems that I am expected to turn out a nude. Well, I'll do one for them... in the transparency of the atmosphere, with such people as we see out there now. They'll pull it to pieces of course, but they can say what they like."

In his *Concert at the Tuileries* he had shown men in frock-coats. But this failed to satisfy him. He wanted to show these men now in a mythological, pastoral setting, beside a nude. He wanted that setting to be full of light, and the air to be transparent, as he *saw* it to be in reality. The nude would be a woman— a real woman, like those bathing in the Seine. But the stridency of the finished picture, with its inevitable effect of incongruity, left him dissatisfied; he felt that there was something arbitrary about the systematic elaboration of the *Déjeuner*. Though he said nothing, he now deepened his inquiry into the effects to be drawn from the transposition of one world into another. He abandoned the men in frock-coats, clearing the stage of everything except the nude herself and a maid-servant, as he had seen them in the *Urbino Venus*. The effect was smoother but no less potent; in the very temple of beauty, in the lofty sphere of art, the sudden appearance of "what we see" was overwhelming. The frock-coats of *Le Déjeuner sur l'herbe* had softened the shock and made the whole scene almost casual; they had scattered what should have been compressed. In the intimacy and silence of her room, Olympia stands out starkly, violently, the shock of her body's acid vividness softened by nothing, intensified, on the contrary, by the white sheets. The colored maid in the shadows is reduced to the clash of her light pink dress against those shadows, and against the coal-black cat beside her. The only other notes that ring out around Olympia are the big flower hanging over her ear, the bouquet and the flower-patterned bedspread; these stress the "still life" quality of the picture. The color-scheme is so bright and dissonant as to drown out all the rest, which thereupon sinks into the consuming silence of poetry. Even in Manet's eyes everything that went into the picture had been obliterated, and the result was in all respects comparable to a still life. Everything in *Olympia* glides towards *indifference* to beauty. What was only a tentative effort in

Le Déjeuner sur l'herbe reaches fulfillment here. With this supreme play of light handled with flawless technical proficiency, modern painting was born.

Thus was majesty retrieved by the suppression of its outward blandishments—a majesty for everyone and no one, for everything and nothing, belonging simply to what *is* by reason of its *being*, and brought home by the power of painting.

MANET'S SECRET

ONE of the most surprising aspects of Manet's new painting was precisely its close connection with dress and costume. In fact, as I see it, costume and painting have developed along parallel lines. At least this is true of masculine dress which, as it gradually lost the majesty that had distinguished it in the 17th century, grew more and more vulgar. It had once been elegant, eloquent, colorful, but fashion relentlessly stilled its eloquence, dimmed its colors. Today men have altogether lost the polish once conferred on them by an inherent sense of dignity and by dress befitting that dignity. Men have chosen—a little reluctantly—to accept the more realistic standards of democratic equality and, finally, to repudiate a majesty presumptuously bestowed by high birth and religious orders. Today even the wealthy man, however elegant his dress, abstains from the ostentation that might differentiate him from his fellows. It is not too much to say that in his very sobriety he defers to a supreme convention which aspires to the absence of convention, and in effect successfully attains that end.

This unobtrusiveness and sobriety—which many men today go to great lengths to observe—did not gain the upper hand without a struggle, and even then were all too often accompanied by hypocrisy and misgivings. From the start, the new trend was openly resisted. At first the bourgeoisie would have none of a world democratically reduced to *what it was*, and man reduced to plain and simple humanity. It is often harder than it seems for us to forgo that idealization of man associated with qualities we call noble, royal, divine. These words carried vital meaning so long as they had a solid basis in political reality. But with the triumph of the bourgeoisie that reality had ceased to exist.

◄ WOMAN WITH A FAN, 1872. (22¾ × 17¾″) LOUVRE, PARIS.

The bourgeoisie thereafter confined them to the realm of art, where it was thought that, undisturbed, they could go on as before upholding the values of a glorious past, whose forms were sacred. Art was not to be harried or impeded by the changes the bourgeoisie had brought about in government, social life, costume and so forth; on the contrary, its lofty realm of divine and noble forms stood intact—all those forms harmoniously, majestically ordered there as they had once been ordered in a now abolished but well-remembered past. Art was only art by virtue of ignoring what we *see*, what we *are*, in the interests of a theatrical imagination parading before the eye such ghosts of a bygone splendor as might console us for the present banality of the world. In the studios the master's byword was not to copy the model as it might really appear...

All his life Manet personally respected that particular notion of elegance which stipulated sobriety in dress. He eschewed those aristocratic fashions which, by the mid-19th century, lingered on as mere uncouthness and pretence in the bourgeoisie. He wanted to, and did, belong to his own time, and dressed and painted accordingly, rejecting outright the anachronisms that screened off reality behind a façade of fiction. Courbet before him had resolutely shown things as they really are, with a gusto that still amazes us. The density and fine vital energy of Courbet's art are undeniable, but his realism had not yet been stripped of eloquence; his art pleads nobly, eloquently, for the truth of things and this nobility is the one relic of a dead past to which Courbet clung. His eloquence, needless to say, had nothing in common with the turgid, highflown, bare-faced lying of conventional art. But it was not yet the laconic elegance, the economy of statement that we do not find till Manet stepped forward—till the day, that is, when the subject, treated with indifference, became a mere pretext for the picture itself.

LE DÉJEUNER A L'ATELIER, 1868-1869. (47¼ × 60½″)
NEUE STAATSGALERIE, MUNICH.

Painted at Boulogne on the Channel Coast, in the dining-room (not in
the atelier) of the house on the waterfront which Manet had rented for
the summer. The tall youth in the foreground is his son-in-law (or son)
Léon Koella. The motley assortment of objects in this interior caught
Manet's fancy for the good reason, very probably, that no existing convention justified such an array. The secret of the picture resides in the curious
fact that the central figure, though he looms large, does not monopolize
attention, which wanders freely over the idly engrossed secondary figures
and the opulent wealth of fine still lifes that so distinguish this canvas.

Manet brought a master's hand to the still life. It was the one subject to which no strings were attached, the one subject intrinsically meaningless; thus he could approach it from a strictly painterly angle, the objects represented being a mere pretext for the act of painting. With Manet the still life came into its own, the play of the brush lending it the same depth that the fund of a great composer's inspiration lends to music.

STILL LIFE WITH SALMON, 1866. (28 × 36")
MRS J. WATSON WEBB COLLECTION, NEW YORK.

What is more, stripped to essentials, Manet's sober elegance almost immediately struck a note of utter integrity by virtue not simply of its indifference to the subject, but of the active self-assurance with which it expressed that indifference. Manet's was *supreme indifference*, effortless and stinging; it scandalized but never deigned to take any notice of the shock it produced. Scandal merely for scandal's sake would have been inelegant, a breach of sobriety. His sobriety was the more complete and efficacious in moving from a passive to an active state. This active, resolute sobriety was the source of Manet's supreme elegance.

There is a seeming contradiction here. I said that the working principle of this elegance was indifference. The stuff indifference is made of—we might say its intensity—is necessarily manifested when it enters actively into play. It often happens that indifference is revealed as a vital force, or the vehicle of a force, otherwise held in check, which finds an outlet through indifference. In Manet's case the pleasure of painting—nothing less than a passion with him—fused with that indifference to subject-matter which opposed him to the mythological world in which Raphael and Titian had felt at home. With Manet the exultation in his sober powers went hand in hand with the sober delights of destroying what was no longer viable in art. Thanks to his technical virtuosity he could work in the silence of complete freedom and, by the same token, in the silence of rigorous, unsparing destruction. *Olympia* was the height of elegance in that both its rarified color-scheme and the negation of a convention-bound world were carried to the same pitch of intensity. Conventions were meaningless here since the subject, whose meaning was cancelled out, was no more than a pretext for the act—the *gamble*—of painting.

THE BALCONY, 1868-1869. (66¼ × 48½") LOUVRE, PARIS. ▶

82

83

Indifference to the subject distinguishes not only Manet's approach to painting, but that of the Impressionists and, with few exceptions, of all modern painters. Monet once said that he would have liked to come into the world blind, and then regain his eyesight, so as to see forms and colors independently of the objects and uses to which, by force of habit, we relate

BOUQUET OF VIOLETS AND FAN, 1872. (8½ × 10½″)
PRIVATE COLLECTION, PARIS.

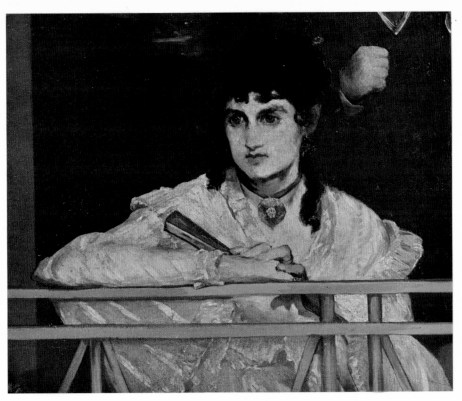

THE BALCONY (DETAIL), 1868-1869. LOUVRE, PARIS.

The reproduction of this detail in close-up does more than focus attention on an admirable portrait of a handsome young woman, whose deep gaze is laden with the sultriness of a day in late summer when a far-off storm is brewing. This detail, in fact, is indispensable to the understanding of a composition so ordered—apparently quite by chance, without the painter's realizing as much—that at first our attention cannot fully be brought to bear on it as a whole. Then, as we begin to take it in, we scent the deep secret behind this picture—the beauty and intensity of life itself.

them. But in the work of Monet and his friends we do not find the passion for silencing that which is naturally moved to speak, and for stripping that which convention clothes. This operation, seen at work in *Olympia*, where its forthright precision is almost magical in effect, makes for Manet's unique charm and distinguishes him from his successors. It gives *Olympia* the pre-eminence that led his friends, in 1889, to purchase it from his widow and offer it to the Louvre, and so strongly did Manet's friends feel about the matter that they grew indignant at the lone dissent of Antonin Proust, who felt *Argenteuil* to be a better picture. But the operation had reached its climax in *Olympia*; there could be no denying that. And if Manet's contribution to the new painting were to be summed up in a single picture, that picture could only be *Olympia*. His friends unhesitatingly singled out the same picture singled out by his enemies for opposite reasons.

I have pointed to a similar operation—of silencing the rhetorical forms of old and stripping them of their conventional baggage—in *The Execution of Maximilian*, in which, perhaps, it is "brought off" less perfectly, but no less plainly than in *Olympia* and *Le Déjeuner sur l'herbe*; its principles were laid down, at least to a point, in *Concert at the Tuileries*. In each, instead of the theatrical forms expected of him, Manet offered up the starkness of "what we see." And each time it so happened that the public's frustrated expectation only redoubled the effect of shocked surprise produced by the picture. That frustrated expectation was one thing, the beauty and daring of Manet's color contrasts another; the former amplified the latter, and it is in the former and not, as Malraux would have it, in "the green of *The Balcony*" or in "the pink patch of *Olympia*" that there resides "the contribution, not necessarily superior, but totally different that Manet made." Malraux is perhaps open

Adolphe Tabarant has shown that this scene took place in a vacant lot in the Rue de l'Estrapade, on the edge of the Mouffetard quarter of Paris. Beyond we can identify the domes of the Observatoire, the Val-de-Grâce, the Panthéon, and the belfry of Saint-Etienne-du-Mont. This funeral of a child under an uncertain sky on ground still streaked with snow dates from early 1870. We know nothing, however, of the mood or circumstances that led up to this painted sketch, so fine in its harsh vigor.

THE FUNERAL, 1870. (28⅝ × 35⅝")
BY COURTESY OF THE METROPOLITAN MUSEUM OF ART, NEW YORK.

to blame for not having stressed the magic workings of the strange, half-hidden operation to which I refer. He grasped the decisive steps taken by Manet, with whom modern painting and its indifference to the subject begin, but he fails to bring out the basic contrast between Manet's attitude and the indifference of the Impressionists towards the subject. He fails to define what gives *Olympia*—which in itself is no finer a picture than several other Manets—its value *as an operation*.

Olympia reveals Manet's secret. Nowhere else is it so patently revealed; but once we see it here we find traces of it in nearly all his works. Manet afterwards did his level best to repeat what he had brought off so successfully in *Olympia*; in his *Portrait of Zacharie Astruc* he even reverted to the background partition he had taken over from Titian's *Urbino Venus*. Elsewhere he resorted to other devices whose purpose was always the same: to frustrate conventional expectations. I think it is safe to say that, in *A l'ombre des jeunes filles en fleur*, Marcel Proust's analysis of Elstir's mannerisms and style really applies to Manet. Elstir himself is not Manet, whom Proust could hardly have known personally as he was only a twelve-year-old boy at the time of Manet's death. But Elstir is not far removed from Manet. Proust spoke of "the period... in which Elstir's personality had not yet fully emerged and still drew inspiration from Manet." This is true in the sense that the character of Elstir in the novel is patterned to some extent after Manet as he was in real life. Proust tacitly admits as much when he says that "Zola wrote a study on Elstir," and again when he specifies that, in addition to his Balbec seascapes, Elstir painted *A Bunch of Asparagus*. These seascapes are anything but imaginary; they are those Manet painted at Boulogne, Berck and elsewhere. The gist of what Proust had to say about them is that where we should expect to see land, the painter shows us water, and then shows land

BALL AT THE OPERA, 1873. (23¾ × 29")
MRS HORACE HAVEMEYER COLLECTION, NEW YORK.

One of the most delightful representations of a festive occasion that any
painter has made, superlatively free of convention and full of cunning
details—the choppy sea of top hats, the three or four black velvet masks
with the bright eyes of gay young women gleaming behind and, most
striking of all, the leg dangling over the balcony in the top of the picture.

where we should expect to see the water. "One of the most frequently recurring metaphors in the seascapes he had near him at the time was precisely his way of likening shore to sea and thereby abolishing all distinction between them. It was his way of drawing this comparison, repeating it implicitly and unwearyingly throughout a given canvas, that imparted to it that powerful, many-sided unity, the source, though not always clearly recognized as such, of the enthusiasm Elstir's painting aroused in certain art-lovers." What Proust is driving at is the unity of visual effect the spectator enjoys as he moves smoothly and easily from one aspect of the subject to another. When Proust alludes to a ship as "some citified, earth-built thing," to what other painting do these words more aptly apply than to Manet's *Folkestone Boat*? This knack of producing the unusual and unexpected by abolishing habitual distinctions between unlike things had an even larger significance for Proust, who wrote: "It sometimes happened in Paris that, from my room, I overheard a dispute, almost a riot, which I went on listening to until I had identified the cause of the uproar, for example a carriage, whose shrill, discordant clamor my ears had really heard, but which until then I had not acknowledged, knowing in my mind that wheels do not produce such sounds." In the writer's mind, as in the painter's, the same transition occurred, the prosaic responses of the mind melting away into sense impressions; both men found this phenomenon far richer, far more inspiring than the inevitable reverse transition from sensibility back to intelligence, and both, whether by instinct or calculation, practised a subtle artistic wizardry that enabled them to recapture all the innocence and freshness of the original impression. We see its effects in *On the Beach*, in which the

THE PIER AT BOULOGNE, 1869. (28 × 36¼″)
PRIVATE COLLECTION, PARIS.

immensity of the figures relegates the sea to insignificance. Or in *The Manet Family at Arcachon*, in which the sea, visible through the open window, overwhelms the room itself.

This disproportion of the picture elements is absent from the general run of impressionist paintings. Unquestionably it was Manet whom Proust had in mind when he described the process.

This view of the sea, in which the steamer is moored alongside the coach on the docks (and might almost be confused with it), recalls the "metaphors" resorted to by the painter Elstir in *A l'ombre des jeunes filles en fleur*, which Marcel Proust no doubt coined with this canvas by Manet in mind. "Those rare moments," wrote Proust, "in which we see nature such as she is, poetically, those were the moments of which Elstir's works were made. One of the most frequently recurring metaphors in the seascapes he had near him at the time was precisely his way of likening shore to sea and thereby abolishing all distinction between them." Manet sometimes painted the world as a "perfect mirage," so that the objects depicted lost all intrinsic value or meaning, becoming mere focal points for the uninhibited play of lights and shadows. The ever-shifting forces of the sea interpenetrate the earth's bulk and produce those lighter images the new art sought to record as it repudiated threadbare conventions and contrived other and subtler means of circumventing the literal and the commonplace.

THE FOLKESTONE BOAT, 1869. (24¾ × 39¾")
OSKAR REINHART COLLECTION, WINTERTHUR.

IN A BOAT, 1874. (37¾ × 51")
HORACE HAVEMEYER COLLECTION, METROPOLITAN MUSEUM OF ART,
NEW YORK.

This picture is the most enthusiastic tribute Manet ever paid to the impressionist ideal of bright-colored canvases painted entirely in the open air. But the work is no less remarkable for the boldness of the lay-out; our realization that the man and woman are boating on a river only comes as an afterthought. This delayed-action effect adds a poetic element of surprise to these figures situated in, yet so distinctly cut off from, the familiar world of the great out-of-doors, and from its color and light. The whole composition breathes energy and refinement at once.

In writing about it he carried it even further than Manet had, since he was expressing not so much what Manet had actually done as the conceptions of the post-impressionist and above all post-Manet painter he himself, Proust, potentially was.

There is something strangely elusive in even the most straightforward of Manet's figure paintings, something that slips away from us in the fragility of *The Fifer*, in the spectral apparition of *Angelina*, in the fond and indefinable tenderness of *The Woman with a Parrot*.

Cunningly divided into distinct parts, *The Balcony* is based so wholly on the divergent stares of three pairs of eyes that we feel ill at ease before them. At first glance we see nothing here but a retreat into the insignificant; only later do we wake up and respond to the sultry, hallucinating, wide-eyed gaze of Berthe Morisot, seated at the railing.

In *Le Déjeuner à l'atelier* the peacefulness of a sunny day suggested by the picture provides a pendant to the "calm before the storm" we sense in *The Balcony*. But the same apparent absence of unity among the objects depicted brings out the underlying unity of insignificant things. If the young man in the straw hat is the center of the picture, this is but a subtly emphatic way of demonstrating the fact that he is of no greater importance than the serving-maid or the bearded gentleman lighting an after-dinner cigar—or, for that matter, than the oysters, the armored helmet or the half-peeled lemon.

Ball at the Opera, according to Mallarmé, is "a work of capital importance in the painter's output, something of a culmination summing up many an earlier effort." The stunning effect of the picture is due to the handling of the figures, reduced to a shapeless crowd. The harmony between the textural richness and the thematic insignificance of this *Ball* is so complete that every figure in it seems quite neutral. These men in

THE SEINE BANKS AT ARGENTEUIL, 1874. (24×39¼")
COLLECTION OF THE DOWAGER LADY ABERCONWAY, LONDON.

their top hats and the costumed women with them are only a hair's breadth from the vulgarity of the cartoons featured in the lighter journals of the period. If they are saved from cheapness, it is only thanks to that active, constructive indifference to the subject typical of Manet, by which he reduced them to mere pretexts for his picture. Their grave dignity resides in their very meaninglessness, brilliantly, masterfully accentuated by an art that turns their frivolity into the byways of profundity.

There are many byways that lead to this profundity and silence, many themes permitting of an unusual, unexpected effect—a one-legged cripple with a pair of crutches hobbling

In September 1875 Manet made a brief trip to Venice where, taking to heart the discreet lesson of Canaletto and Guardi, he added the magic touch of art to the magic beauties of that unique city. He brought back two canvases with him to Paris, both frankly impressionist in technique, both painted in the open air. In them nothing remains of the "picturesque" side of Venice save the quintessence of its happy light and colors. Manet beautifully reconciled the principle of painting for its own sake with the "portrait" of a city in which everything combines to provide a feast for the eyes.

THE GRAND CANAL IN VENICE, 1875. (22 × 29")
MRS J. WATSON WEBB COLLECTION, NEW YORK.

THE RUE MOSNIER DECKED OUT WITH FLAGS, 1878. (25 ½ × 31 ¾ ″)
JAKOB GOLDSCHMIDT COLLECTION, NEW YORK.

along a nearly deserted street made gay with holiday bunting, or the same street torn up by pavers, or simply a close-up of people in a busy café.

For the last time—though stricken with locomotor ataxy, which soon proved fatal—Manet painted a large composition in which no empty spaces were left. *Un Bar aux Folies-Bergère*

STREET PAVERS IN THE RUE MOSNIER, 1878. (24¾ × 31″)
MR R.A. BUTLER COLLECTION, LONDON.

is a bewitching interplay of lights gleaming in a vast mirror.
Bottles, fruit and flowers stand in full light to either side of
the barmaid, a tall handsome girl, but strangely lusterless, her
eyes clouded with fatigue or boredom beneath her blond bangs.
The crowd, really in front of her, is only a reflected image
dancing in the luminous wonderland of the mirror behind.

AT THE CAFÉ, 1878. $(18\frac{5}{8} \times 15\frac{3}{8}'')$
WALTERS ART GALLERY, BALTIMORE.

FROM DOUBT TO THE SUPREME VALUE

IT must be added that, whatever the light thrown on it, Manet's secret elucidates not the whole problem, but only a part of it. That part, moreover, is quite capable of preventing us from grasping the whole which it completes and perhaps even explains, but for which it cannot be substituted. Manet, after all, is only one man in a great lineage of French painters running uninterruptedly from David to Courbet. It might plausibly be maintained that Monet, Renoir, Cézanne, and perhaps even Degas, though in the main they share the same tradition, depart from it to some extent, whereas Manet is an integral part of it. If we set aside Ingres and Corot, with whom he has hardly any noticeable affinity, Manet obviously belongs to the age of Daumier and Courbet, who—rather than Delacroix —were his most immediate predecessors. There can be no question about his admiration for Delacroix; he figures alongside Baudelaire in Fantin-Latour's *Homage to Delacroix*. But Manet made certain reservations none the less. He turned his back on historical painting once for all and looked with some suspicion upon Delacroix's warm, tumultuous colors. Even so, it cannot be said that the latter's delight in the passionate handling of the paints had any secrets for Manet, who, as Mallarmé records, "flung himself at the canvas, pell-mell, as if he had never painted before." But his tastes inclined him to harmonies which, for being full-bodied, were no less muffled and subdued, a reticence which the painter, like the pianist with a predilection for the soft pedal, only achieves through a mastery verging on coldness and insensitivity. Just as his powers were reaching their peak, Manet's abhorrence of facile lyricism and muddy depths moved him to adopt those flat colors which came as a complete surprise to his contemporaries and led his detractors to complain that his figures were "no thicker than playing cards." *The Fifer* is the most compelling example of such "playing-card pictures," but all Manet's aspirations headed him in the same direction: toward forms and colors which at times are almost sere, stiff, leaden-hued, handled vehemently perhaps, but always productive of that elegant thinness of the pictorial image, that flat transparency which sounded the death-knell of rhetorical eloquence in painting.

Strictly speaking, this was but an extension of the painting of the past. It had no share in that wealth of color that characterized Impressionism. On the contrary, it was an impoverished version of the past, which it whittled down to ordinary proportions, to a stark, well-defined simplicity.

Judged solely in terms of the vibration of color on canvas, Manet is not the greatest painter of his day. Both Delacroix and Courbet have a breadth and an easy, all-embracing power which he lacks, while Corot too had a deeper grasp of simple, elusive truths. Manet's manner, less sure of itself, proceeds from a more aggressive and less wholesome impulsion. Manet sows the seeds of unrest and has no wish to satisfy; he deliberately sets out to baffle and disturb. He is unwilling to concede what has always been taken for granted: that the picture is meant to represent something. His art is an extension of that of his elders, but with him an exasperation enters into the act of painting, a fever comes over him that sets him groping for the fluke or the random effect that widens or overshoots the usual limits of the picture. Manet's virtuosity has its ties with that of French painting in his time, which was rich in possibilities and avid of new values; but his was distinguished by oblique forays into the unknown and abrupt violations of accepted values. His emphatic use of flat colors and the outright suppression of intermediate shadings, though without any intrinsic significance, were necessary innovations that cleared the air; they extricated painting from the quagmire of rhetoric in which it had long

been bogged down and tided it over till such time as the subject expected of the painter had ceased to be anything but an unexpected, an unforeseeable sensation, a pure, high-pitched vibration to which no particular meaning could be assigned.

Above all else paintings were formerly required to have "finish," and this it was that consecrated the value inherent in the subject of the picture. Manet, however, found that he could get finer effects in the "sketch" of a picture than in a highly finished work. Such effects thereupon became, as Lionello Venturi puts it, a kind of "finite of the non-finite," something of far more meaning and consequence than the most minutely wrought canvas. Speaking of Manet, Mallarmé declared that it made no difference whether one of his works were entirely finished or not, there being "a harmony amongst all its elements by virtue of which it holds together and possesses a charm easily broken by the addition of a single brushstroke."

I would stress the fact that what counts in Manet's canvases is not the subject, but the vibration of light. The role of light in his art is more complex than is implied either by Malraux's analysis of Manet or by those who see the apotheosis of light in the impressionist technique. To break up the subject and re-establish it on a different basis is not to neglect the subject; so it is in a sacrifice, which takes liberties with the victim and even kills it, but cannot be said to *neglect* it. After all, the subject in Manet's pictures is not so much "killed" as simply overshot, outdistanced; not so much obliterated in the interests of pure painting as transfigured by the stark purity of that painting. A whole world of pictorial research is contained in the singularity of his subjects. Does Manet lie at the origin of Impressionism? Possibly, but all the same his painting arose out of depths of which Impressionism had no inkling. No painter more heavily invested the subject, not with meaning, but with that which goes beyond and is more significant than meaning.

Manet 44

ASPARAGUS, 1880. $(6\frac{1}{2} \times 8\frac{1}{2}")$
SAM SALZ COLLECTION, NEW YORK.

When Manet painted *A Bunch of Asparagus*, Charles Ephrussi not only bought the picture from him but gave him 200 francs more than he asked (which represents some 40,000 French francs—well over 100 dollars—in present-day money). To thank him Manet painted this *Asparagus* and sent it to his friend as a surprise. "There was one missing from the bunch I gave you," he wrote in the accompanying letter. Here we have the playful side of Manet's temperament; he never felt happier than when he could defeat the conventions attaching to a given genre of painting without lapsing into arbitrariness—and here he defeated them with complete success.

It must be conceded that at first sight his still lifes do not seem to convey this higher meaning. Yet meaninglessness of sorts is the peculiar privilege of the still life, which had always been accepted as introducing something of a void, a purely decorative pause, into the significant whole of which painting and indeed all art were so important a part. The still life played

TWO ROSES ON A TABLECLOTH, 1882-1883. (7¼ × 9½ ″)
MR AND MRS WILLIAM S. PALEY COLLECTION, NEW YORK.

no part in the prevailing order of values, but served as no more than a humble decorative element in the capitals of churches.

Manet's splendid still lifes are quite unlike the decorative *hors-d'œuvre* of the past. They are pictures in their own right, since Manet, from the very start, had put the image of man on the same footing as that of roses or buns. Yet in *Le Déjeuner à l'atelier*, for example, the inert objects on the chair and table are raised to the level of the human figures to the same extent that the latter are reduced to the level of things. In this particular reciprocity of meanings and importances—but in this particular reciprocity only—Malraux is justified in observing that "it is no accident if Manet is above all a great still life painter." An element of vague raillery, perhaps stemming from the momentary aggressiveness of his style, nevertheless enters into these indifferent objects. Manet's still lifes are not yet imbued with that "secret royalty" which Malraux rightly attributes to Cézanne's. Manet's lemons are incongruous. That incongruity is acutely intensified in *The Asparagus*, which reveals the full depth of Manet's indifference to the subject.

By reason of his early death Manet left a relatively small number of paintings behind him, but such is their variety that it is no easy matter to grasp their general pattern or describe them in a few words. All that emerges is that personal touch by which, at a single glance, we recognize a Manet, just as we recognize, for example, a Cézanne or a Seurat. But the extreme diversity of his work virtually belies that "personal touch" which, in a manner of speaking, sums up Manet in our minds. And even if not quite belying it, that diversity literally invalidates it, for it is the aftermath of the artist's original uncertainty as to the exact nature of his future canvases or of his work as a whole, so perfectly rounded off in retrospect by the death of the painter himself. We admire one of his pictures as it hangs on the wall, but it is something else again to imagine that picture

PORTRAIT OF MADEMOISELLE GAUTHIER-LATHUILLE, 1879. (24 × 19¾″)
MUSÉE DES BEAUX-ARTS, LYONS.

WOMAN FIXING HER GARTER, 1878. (20¾ × 17¼″) PASTEL.
WILHELM HANSEN COLLECTION, DANISH STATE MUSEUM, ORDRUPGAARD.

as it first existed, hovering between the uncertainty it was for the painter and the certainty it is for us. With Manet in particular, who never clearly knew what he wanted, who was less sure of himself than most artists are, and who, far from plotting out a course for himself and sticking to it, was forever searching for his way, harried by doubts and fearful of the opinions of others—with him in particular, how can we avoid stressing that element of blind chance which tips the scales one way or the other, and which only rash self-confidence or fatigue allows the artist to forget? If we do not view these highly varied paintings in the original light in which they came into being, how mistaken we may be about them!

Are not indecision and hesitation the essential ingredients of Manet's charm? Had it not been for Berthe Morisot, in whom he discovered the double enchantment of a painter's talents and a model's beauty, he might never have tried his hand at impressionist painting. Until they met Manet had painted only somber canvases, and had always worked inside the studio. He had never seriously considered the new methods of the young men who till then had been no more than his admirers and cronies at the Café Guerbois. Berthe Morisot alone prompted him to go out-of-doors and paint in bright colors—to practise what the Impressionists called *peinture claire*; the result was, in his middle period, *In a Boat*, the Argenteuil pictures, *Monet painting in his Boat* and *The Grand Canal in Venice*. But if it is true he revised his methods, Manet always held aloof from Impressionism. When in 1874 his friends, to a man, withdrew from the Salon competition and organized the First Group Exhibition of the Impressionists, Manet refused to join them. At the end of 1874 Berthe Morisot married his brother Eugène and thereafter ceased posing for him. Actually Manet's impressionist venture came to an end with her marriage, though later, during his fatal illness, his stays at Bellevue, Versailles and Rueil led him back to the open air of country gardens; then he painted *The Promenade*, into which the imminence of death infused an abandon and simplicity that he had hitherto eschewed.

Unstable, hesitant, always on edge and tortured by doubt—that is the only image, a far cry from placid indifference, which I can form of Manet. Essentially erratic and trembling in its course, betraying some secret inclination of its own, his hand never yielded to the conventional dictates that might have been inspired by the subject. Painting, if it is to be independent of all that is not painting, inevitably reveals the inmost being of the man whose hand and brain drive the brush. *Joie de vivre* lights up every painting by Monet and Renoir, while cynicism puts a cold stare in Degas' eye. Indifference erected into a principle signifies the decision to avoid expressing in a picture anything that can possibly be expressed in words. But Manet's deepest feelings never ceased to be expressed on canvas.

Boy with a Dog, perhaps his first masterpiece, communicates an indefinable sadness which is apparently bound up with the death of the youngster who had posed for *Boy with Cherries*. The latter had been employed by Manet to clean his brushes and scrape his palettes, and occasionally served as a model, but, having dawdled over his chores and been reprimanded, he hanged himself; Baudelaire's *La Corde* relates this tragic incident. It affected Manet with fits of melancholy contrasting with the sunny cheerfulness which, according to his friend De Nittis, the Italian painter, was Manet's true temperament.

Add to this the rankling sensuality that makes itself felt in certain pictures. No doubt it only lurks in the background of *Olympia*, but it is there, nevertheless, in the almost obsessive nudity of the girl. *Un Bar aux Folies-Bergère* is an explosive festival of light, overrunning and absorbing the girl's motionless

NANA, 1877. (59 × 45 ½ ") KUNSTHALLE, HAMBURG. ▶

beauty; but a sly, underhand moral complacency weighs heavy on this picture. In *Ball at the Opera* we find the same equivocal mingling of restraint and licentiousness. The color magic of all these paintings is potent enough to make up for the meagerness of the subject. This is not the case with *Nana*, which, though a masterful performance, is essentially cold and lifeless.

UN BAR AUX FOLIES-BERGÈRE, 1881. (37¾×51″)
SAMUEL COURTAULD COLLECTION, LONDON.

The model of *Nana*, Henriette Hauser, was one of the many women Manet met at Tortoni's and elsewhere, whose company he enjoyed and of whom he made a number of portraits. Of these women Méry Laurent, first Mallarmé's mistress, then Manet's, was the best known and certainly the most charming. *Nana* is distinguished by a provocative *mise en scène* as highly modern as that expressed in terms of modern dress in *Concert at the Tuileries*; later interpreted as an illustration for Zola's novel, it was not originally intended as such. It was nevertheless a genre scene, tending towards the anecdote, just as *At the Café* was to be after it. Such works as these opened the door to concessions.

These concessions, however, were never a betrayal of Manet's basic principles. He never painted anything else but "what he saw." The picture he exhibited at the 1861 Salon, the *Portrait of M. and Mme Auguste Manet* (his parents), a picture that literally cries out the truth and integrity behind it, is but a poor example of that subversive type of painting that was soon to be nothing less than a blind passion with Manet. Perhaps he occasionally felt the need of a breathing-spell, a respite, in the hostility that surrounded him. Yet, even then, he never painted a picture that could be described as unworthy of him, despite such works as *Le bon bock*, which in 1873 inaugurated a series of realistic genre scenes calculated to please the public. This picturesque and amiable figure completely deprived his detractors of their chief argument, to the effect that Manet did not really know how to paint. *Chez le père Lathuille*, coming a little later, suggests that Manet deliberately tried his hand at being a painter of the picturesque and quaint truly in the spirit of his time. This tendency appears in a number of his later canvases: *Nana*, *At the Café*, perhaps even *The Wash*, *La Serveuse de bocks* and *In the Greenhouse*. None of these paintings would be out of place in an illustrated edition of Maupassant.

THE GARDEN AT BELLEVUE, 1880. (21¼ × 25½″)
PRIVATE COLLECTION, PARIS.

Towards the end of his life, as the symptoms of illness grew, Manet summered each year in the villages outside Paris. There he relished the best of life—a summer's day in the garden, a woman's beauty—and a fresh radiance colors these visions of a dying man, no longer wrapped up in supersubtle investigations, but exulting in an impressionist *joie de vivre*.

THE PROMENADE, 1880. (36½ × 27½″)
JAKOB GOLDSCHMIDT COLLECTION, NEW YORK. ▶

It would be a mistake to magnify these apparent "short-comings." Neither Manet's abilities nor his utter sincerity can be called into doubt. Even though related to this later group of pictures, *Un Bar aux Folies-Bergère*, which dates from 1881, somehow casts a spell by which it is completely transfigured. *The Suicide*—no less rigid and mute than *The Execution of Maximilian*—together with many portraits and all the late still lifes have an irresistible charm about them. This is especially true of the *Portrait of Mallarmé*, painted about the same time as *Nana*; after *Olympia* it is Manet's masterpiece.

If by and large a rule of silence is imposed throughout Manet's work, the *Portrait of Mallarmé* is an exception. Its eloquence is discreet, but it is eloquent none the less. What is more, this portrait carries a meaning; it signifies in painting what Mallarmé signifies in poetry. "In order to paint his *Portrait of Clemenceau*," writes Malraux, "Manet had to make up his mind to put the whole of himself into it, and practically nothing of Clemenceau." The same cannot be said of the *Portrait of Mallarmé*.

In his important book on Manet (written in collaboration with Georges Wildenstein and M.L. Bataille) Paul Jamot, who was studying English under Mallarmé's instruction at the time, tells how deeply he was struck by the likeness of the portrait. But profounder considerations than this attach the portrait to Mallarmé. The evasive eyes, turning about the room with an almost fugue-like movement; the face, freed of all heaviness by the sketchwise treatment; the drifting of attention, yet the intensely concentrated gaze; the impression of calm dizziness —is all this the reflection on canvas of Manet's own emotional responses? That well may be, but before all else these rigorous

PORTRAIT OF GEORGE MOORE, 1879. (21½ × 13″)   PASTEL.   ►
HORACE HAVEMEYER COLLECTION, METROPOLITAN MUSEUM OF ART, NEW YORK.

117

forms, which almost seem to mirror the undulating, weightless rapidity of birdflight, and these austere harmonies of pale blue are intimately connected with Mallarmé. This interplay of forms and colors is not the painter's alone, but owes a large debt of expression to Mallarmé himself.

Does this picture contradict the principle of indifference inherent in Manet's canvases? It would be more accurate, I think, to say that nothing in the *Mallarmé* disturbs the feeling of stark pictorial integrity we get from Manet's masterpieces. It does not belie, but rather discloses, that supreme value which is the true goal of painting, of the new art at last stripped free of the pathetic shadows the art of the past had labored to perpetuate. The *artist*, if he is Mallarmé, is the very incarnation of art. Manet, understandably, had no wish to abolish the meaning of such a subject as that.

This remarkable portrait is a model of what the art of painting can be—painting plumbed to the depths and stripped of vain ornaments. What completely transfigures the work is that supreme value which for a century had been a ghostly presence in the studios but which no artist had quite been capable of capturing. Valéry attributed what he called "Manet's triumph" to the stimulus of poetry in the person first of Baudelaire, then of Mallarmé. This "triumph," it seems to me, reaches fulfillment in the *Portrait of Mallarmé*.

I see the hand of destiny in the meeting of these two men, both in pursuit of the same ideals, Manet in paints, Mallarmé in words. Manet's portrait of him reduced the poet, at least in a manner of speaking, to that caprice, grave and light-hearted at once, which we find in his poems. The touch of his

ROSES AND LILACS, 1882-1883. (21 ½ × 13 ¾ ")
MR AND MRS EDWIN C. VOGEL COLLECTION, NEW YORK.

►

brush on the canvas was both light and firm, tenuous and emphatic; thus he conveyed his most elusive and subtle impressions. Something of this ingenious avoidance of plain and literal expression remains in the *Portrait of George Moore*. Perhaps never has the human face been treated as a still life more convincingly than here.

These two portraits are worlds away from those Manet made of other friends whose characters, he probably felt, lacked that particular transparency which, above all, he sought to render. In connection with the *Portrait of Théodore Duret*, for example, I might again speak of the meaninglessness of the still life, were it not that the smug apathy of the man himself—Duret's personality not being that of an artist—succeeds in defeating this tendency and the portrait, of itself, dwindles to an unsuggestive play of forms and colors. The portraits of Antonin Proust and Clemenceau add some nuances to these humanized still lifes, but their personalities are completely neutralized by the marvelous and capricious powers of Manet's brush. And if the two portraits of Astruc and Zola—whom Manet certainly should have regarded as artists—seem to differ from the rest, that, I believe, is because they are less accomplished paintings.

Earlier, in *The Balcony*, we noticed a similar case of contrast between vacant faces and a face charged with subtle sensibility. In that picture, actually three portraits in one, the vacancy of Antoine Guillemet and Fanny Claus acts as a neutral setting for Berthe Morisot's jewel-like face, lit up from within by the combined glow of art and feminine beauty.

In the many portraits of attractive women Manet painted during his last period, the subject, admittedly, is stated and defined with anything but reticence; *The Balcony* was the first of such pictures and was followed not only by the portraits of contemporary beauties but also by the *Portrait of Mallarmé*.

As for all the earlier pictures for which Victorine Meurend posed, including *Olympia*, their appeal lay elsewhere; their surface charms were literally crushed to extinction beneath the massive *absence* of meaning conveyed by the picture as a whole. Then, quite unexpectedly, the figure of Berthe Morisot in *The Balcony* rose like a star calmly sailing amidst the clouds of a night sky. She afterwards appeared again, investing the canvas with a fugitive presence, almost as if there were something unseasonable or unwarranted about its being there, and as if it were about to hasten away again and vanish with the winds. And this is so because, to gain initial entry into Manet's work, a real *subject* had to slip its subrepticious way into the ambiguity of *The Balcony* or, in other portraits, into the tremor of their suspended animation, or, stranger still, in between the spokes of an outspread fan through which nothing is visible but a pair of mysterious eyes.

If it is true, as I believe, that Manet's initial secret is to be discerned in *Olympia*, that transposition of a Renaissance Venus, there is a deeper secret, perhaps, whose hiding-place is hinted at by the outspread fan that conceals it.

What I had hoped to show in Manet was one of the most reticent painters of recent times, whose work is exceptionally difficult of access. In all respects he was the man best qualified to herald the birth of that wonderland, so full of delights and surprises, which, today, modern painting offers up to our gaze.

SELECTED BIBLIOGRAPHY

CHIEF EXHIBITIONS

INDEX OF NAMES

CONTENTS

SELECTED BIBLIOGRAPHY

Catalogues and Standard Works

A. Tabarant, *Histoire catalographique*, Paris 1931; id., *Manet et ses œuvres*, Paris 1947. — P. Jamot, G. Wildenstein, M. L. Bataille, *Manet*, 2 vols., Paris 1932 (catalogue of 546 items, 487 illustrations, with an introduction by P. Jamot and a chronological survey, an index and an exhaustive bibliography). — M. Guerin, *L'œuvre gravé de Manet*, Paris 1944 (new enlarged edition of E. Moreau-Nélaton's *Manet graveur et lithographe*, Paris 1906).

Manet's Letters

T. Duret, *Quelques lettres de Manet et Sisley*, in *La Revue Blanche*, Paris, March 15, 1899. — E. Manet, *Lettres de jeunesse (1848-1849)*, *Voyage à Rio*, Paris 1929. — J. Guiffrey, *Lettres illustrées d'Edouard Manet*, Paris 1929. — A. Tabarant, *Une correspondance inédite d'Edouard Manet. Lettres du Siège de Paris*, Paris 1935. — *Lettres d'Edouard Manet sur son voyage en Espagne*, in *Arts*, Paris, March 16, 1945.

Reminiscences

G. Moore, *Confessions of a Young Man*, London 1888; id., *Memoirs of my Dead Life*, London 1906. — G. De Nittis, *Notes et Souvenirs*, Paris 1895. — A. Proust, *Souvenirs de Manet*, in *La Revue Blanche*, Paris 1897; id., *Edouard Manet, Souvenirs*, Paris 1913. — J. E. Blanche, *Essais et portraits*, Paris 1912. — P. Courthion, *Manet raconté par lui-même et par ses amis*, Geneva 1945 (new edition in 2 vols., Geneva 1954).

Monographs and Critical Studies

Z. Astruc, *Le Salon intime : Exposition du Boulevard des Italiens*, Paris 1860; id., *Le Salon*, Paris 1863. — E. Zola, *Mon Salon*, Paris 1866; id., *Edouard Manet, Etude biographique et critique*, Paris 1867 (incorporated in *Mes Haines*, Paris 1902). — W. Bürger (Thoré-Bürger), *Salons (de 1861 et 1868)*, Paris 1870. — A. Castagnary, *Salons (de 1857 à 1879)*, Paris

1892. — P. Duranty, *La Nouvelle Peinture*, Paris 1876; id., *Le Pays des Arts*, Paris 1881. — J. K. Huysmans, *L'Art moderne, Salon (de 1879), Exposition des Indépendants en 1881, Salon (de 1881)*, Paris 1883. — E. Bazire, *Manet*, Paris 1884. — J. de Bietz, *Edouard Manet* (lecture), Paris 1884. — F. Fénéon, *Les impressionnistes en 1886*, Paris 1886. — S. Mallarmé, *Divagations*, Paris 1898. — G. Moore, *Modern Painting*, London 1898. — T. Duret, *Histoire d'Edouard Manet et de son œuvre*, Paris 1902 (reprinted many times); id., *Manet and the French Impressionists*, London & Philadelphia 1910. — H. von Tschudi, *Edouard Manet*, Berlin 1902. — J. Meier-Graefe, *Manet und sein Kreis*, Berlin 1903; id., *Edouard Manet*, Munich 1912. — C. Mauclair, *L'Impressionnisme, son histoire, son esthétique, ses maîtres*, Paris 1904. — L. Hourticq & L. Laran, *Manet*, Paris 1912. — E. Waldmann, *Edouard Manet, sein Leben und seine Kunst*, Berlin 1910 & 1923. — J. E. Blanche, *Propos de peintres, de David à Degas*, 1st series, Paris 1919; id., *Manet*, Paris 1924; id., *Manet*, Paris & New York 1925; id., *Les arts plastiques*, Paris 1931. — C. Glaser, *Edouard Manet*, Munich 1922. — G. Severini, *Edouard Manet*, Rome 1924. — L. Rosenthal, *Manet aquafortiste et lithographe*, Paris 1925. — E. Moreau-Nélaton, *Manet raconté par lui-même*, 2 vols., with 353 reproductions, Paris 1926 (fundamental). — T. Duret, *Manet y España*, Paris 1927. — *Manet*, Marées Gesellschaft, Munich 1928. — A. Flament, *La Vie de Manet*, Paris 1928. — C. V. Wheeler, *Manet, An Essay*, Washington 1930. — C. Léger, *Manet*, Paris 1931. — P. Colin, *Manet*, Paris 1932. — P. Valéry, *Le Triomphe de Manet*, preface to the Manet Retrospective Exhibition at the Musée de l'Orangerie, Paris 1932 (incorporated in *Pièces sur l'art*, Paris 1932). — R. Rey, *Choix de 65 dessins de Manet*, Paris 1932; id., *Manet*, Paris 1938. — W. George, *Manet et la carence du spirituel*, Paris 1932. — A. Tabarant, *Manet*, Paris 1939. — G. Jedlicka, *Manet*, Zurich 1941. — H. Graber, *Edouard Manet nach eigenen und fremden Zeugnissen*, Basel 1941. — R. Mortimer, *Edouard Manet, "Un Bar aux Folies-Bergère"*, London (1944). — L. Piérard, *Manet l'incompris*, Paris 1946. — J. Rewald, *Edouard Manet, Pastels*, Oxford 1947. — M. Florisoone, *Manet*, Monaco 1947. — B. Reifenberg, *Manet*, Bern 1947. — J. Alazard, *Manet*, Lausanne 1948. — J. Leymarie, *Manet et les impressionnistes au Musée du Louvre*, Paris 1948; id., *Manet*, Paris 1952. — M. Bex, *Manet*, Paris 1948. — H. Dumont, *Manet*, Paris 1949. — F. Mathey, introduction to *Edouard Manet, peintures*, Paris 1949. — A. van Anrooy, *Impromptu* (with regard to Manet's marriage), Geneva-Annemasse 1949. — L. Venturi, *Impressionists and Symbolists*, New York 1950; French edition: *De Manet à Lautrec*, Paris 1953. — C. Roger-Marx, *Eva Gonzalès*, Saint-Germain-en-Laye, 1951. — R. Cogniat, introduction and notes to *Manet*, Paris 1953. — J Cassou, *Manet*, Paris 1954 — G. H. Hamilton, *Manet and his Critics*, New Haven & London 1954 — N. G. Sandblad, *Manet, Three Studies in Artistic Conception*, Lund 1954 — F. Daulte, *Le dessin français de Manet à Cézanne*, Paris 1955.

Magazine and Newspaper Articles

T. GAUTIER, *Salon*, in *Le Moniteur Universel*, Paris, July 3, 1861. — E. ZOLA, *Edouard Manet*, in *L'Evénement Illustré*, Paris, May 10, 1868. — A. CASTAGNARY, *Salon*, in *Le Siècle*, Paris, June 11, 1869. — E. DURANTY, *Salon*, in *Paris-Journal*, May 30, 1872; id., *Réflexions d'un bourgeois sur le Salon de peinture*, in *Gazette des Beaux-Arts*, Paris, July 1877. — S. MALLARMÉ, *Le Jury de Peinture pour 1874 et M. Manet*, in *La Renaissance Artistique et Littéraire*, Paris, April 12, 1874. — H. GUÉRARD, *Edouard Manet*, in *Le Carillon*, Paris, July 10, 1881. — G. JEANNIOT, *Manet*, in *La Grande Revue*, Paris, January 1882. — A. PROUST, *Le Salon*, in *Gazette des Beaux-Arts*, Paris 1882; id., *The Art of Edouard Manet*, in *The Studio*, London, January 15, 1901. — P. MANTZ, *Les œuvres de Manet*, in *Le Temps*, Paris, January 16, 1884. — R. MARX, *Edouard Manet et son exposition*, in *Journal des Arts*, Paris, January 11, 1884. — L. GONSE, *Manet*, in *Gazette des Beaux-Arts*, Paris 1884. — R. BOUGER, *L'art nouveau du plein air. L'in-fluence de Manet*, in *Revue Historique Contemporaine*, Paris, May 2, 1891. — G. GEFFROY, *Edouard Manet*, in *La Vie Artistique*, Paris, 1st series 1892 ; 3rd series, 1894; 6th series, 1900. — V. PIVA, *Edouard Manet*, in *Emporium*, May 1907. — G. SÉAILLES, *Edouard Manet*, in *Revue de Paris*, Paris, February 1910. — T. DURET, *Les portraits peints par Manet et refusés par leurs modèles*, in *La Renaissance*, Paris, July 1918. — P. JAMOT, *Manet as a Portrait Painter*, in *The Burlington Magazine*, London, December 1926; id., *Manet, peintre de marines et autres études*, in *Gazette des Beaux-Arts*, Paris 1927; id., *Le Fifre et Victorine Meurend*, in *Revue de l'Art ancien et moderne*, Paris, January 1927. — H. FOCILLON, *Manet en blanc et noir*, in *Gazette des Beaux-Arts*, Paris, December 1927. — P. JAMOT, *Etudes sur Manet*, in *Gazette des Beaux-Arts*, Paris, January & June 1927. — L. VENTURI, *Manet*, in *L'Arte*, 1929. — E. LAMBERT, *Manet et l'Espagne*, in *Gazette des Beaux-Arts*, Paris 1933. — J. MESNIL, *Le Déjeuner sur l'herbe*, in *L'Arte*, 1934. — M. FLORISOONE, *Manet inspiré par Venise*, in *L'Amour de l'Art*, Paris, January 1937. — I. N. EDIN, *Manet and Zola*, in *Gazette des Beaux-Arts*, Paris, June 1945. — J. THYIS, *Manet et Baudelaire*, in *Études d'Art*, Algiers 1945. — J. C. SLOANE, *Manet and History*, in *The Art Quarterly*, vol. 14, 1951.

Special numbers devoted to Manet: *Journal des Curieux*, Paris 1907. — *L'Art et les Artistes*, Paris, October 1930 (article by P. FIERENS). — *L'Amour de l'Art*, Paris, May 1932 (articles by P. JAMOT, G. BAZIN, R. HUYGHE). — *Art Vivant*, June 1932 (article by P. VALÉRY, J. E. BLANCHE, F. FELS, J. GUENNE). — *Formes*, 1932 (articles by J. MEIER-GRAEFE, J. E. BLANCHE, E. JALOUX, M. DORMOY). — *L'Amour de l'Art*, 1947, no. 3-4 (articles by G. BAZIN, M. FLORISOONE, J. LEYMARIE).

CHIEF EXHIBITIONS

Galerie Louis Martinet, Paris, 1861; March 1862; February 1865. — Private Exhibition in a pavilion near the Place de l'Alma, Paris, during the World's Fair, 1867. — *New Works by Edouard Manet*, one-man show in the offices of "La Vie Moderne," Paris, organized by the publisher Charpentier (26 canvases), Paris, April 10-30, 1880. — Posthumous Exhibition at the Ecole Nationale des Beaux-Arts (154 paintings, 22 etchings, 5 lithographs, 13 drawings; preface by Emile Zola), Paris, June 5-28, 1884. — *Manet Retrospective Exhibition* (26 items) at the Salon d'Automne, Paris, October 18-November 25, 1905. — Galerie Durand-Ruel (24 paintings and watercolors), Paris, March 1906. — Galerie Matthiesen, Berlin, February-March 1928. — *Exposition pour les Amis du Luxembourg* (150 items; preface by P. VALÉRY, introduction by P. JAMOT, catalogue by C. STERLING), Paris 1928. — George Wildenstein Gallery (88 items), February 26-April 3, New York 1948.

INDEX OF NAMES

CONTENTS

On the Jacket:

The Promenade, 1880. (36½ × 27½") Jakob Goldschmidt Collection, New York.

*Two Roses on a Tablecloth, 1882-1883. (7¼ × 9½")
Mr and Mrs William S. Paley Collection, New York.*

135

THIS VOLUME
THE FOURTEENTH OF THE COLLECTION

THE TASTE OF OUR TIME

WAS PRINTED
BOTH TEXT AND COLORPLATES
BY THE

SKIRA

COLOR STUDIO
AT IMPRIMERIES RÉUNIES S. A., LAUSANNE
FINISHED THE FIFTEENTH DAY OF SEPTEMBER
NINETEEN HUNDRED AND FIFTY-FIVE

THE PLATES WERE ENGRAVED BY
GUEZELLE & RENOUARD, PARIS

The works reproduced in this volume were photographed by Louis Laniepce, Paris
(pages 16, 20, 28, 33, 48, 68, 73, 76, 83, 84, 85, 90, 92, 96, 99, 107, 108, 114),
by Hans Hinz, Basel (pages 3, 79, 80, 93),
by Henry B. Beville, Washington (pages 23, 32, 34, 37, 39, 40, 41, 44, 46, 47, 57, 81, 87,
89, 97, 98, 100, 104, 105, 115, 117, 119).
Other photographs were obligingly lent
by the magazine Du, Zurich (pages 21, 25, 53, 65, 111),
by Editions Pierre Tisné, Paris (page 112),
and by the Istituto d'Arti grafiche, Bergamo (page 29).

PRINTED IN SWITZERLAND